BIBLIOGRAPHY ON TRIBAL STUDIES

BIBLIOGRAPHY ON TRIBAL STUDIES

GINA SHANGKHAM
RAJENDRA KSHETRI
MUTUM BOKUL SINGH
MEINAM BINOTA DEVI
HENRY BUANGAM
CAROLINE ZOTHANGMAWI

CENTRE FOR MANIPUR STUDIES
MANIPUR UNIVERSITY IMPHAL
AND
AKANSHA PUBLISHING HOUSE
NEW DELHI-110002

AKANSHA PUBLISHING HOUSE
4649-B/21, Ansari Road
Darya Ganj, New Delhi - 110 002
Email: ektabooks@yahoo.com
Ph. : 23263193 / 9811582579

Bibliography on Tribal Studies

First Publisher 2006
ISBN 81-8370-040-3

PRINTED IN INDIA

Published by M.P. Misra for Akansha Publishing House, New Delhi and Printed at Mehra Offset Press, Delhi.

MANIPUR UNIVERSITY
CANCHIPUR
IMPHAL-795 003
MANIPUR. INDIA

Vice-Chancellor

From the Vice-Chancellor's Desk

I am glad to introduce the monograph series on history, culture, ethnography and polity of Manipur, brought out by the Centre for Manipur Studies.

This volume, **A Bibliography of Tribal Studies**, lists all the works done by the researches on Tribal Studies. I am sure that this bibliography will be of immense interest to all the scholars and researchers on Tribal Studies.

N BIJOY SINGH
Vice-Chancellor

Director's Note

The Bibliography on Tribal Studies is a joint venture of a group of research scholars of the Centre for Tribal Studies under the supervision of Prof. Gangmumei Kamei, the then Co-ordinator of the Centre. It is, indeed, a monumental work of the Centre. It is true that Tribal Studies are now one of the most important areas of social science research. A lot of works have been done so far by different writers on various aspects of tribal life an their culture. Their findings give an encouraging contribution in the field of the social science research.

Many people also have written a number of research papers and books on the life and culture of the various tribal people of North East India including Manipur. Their findings were published in the form of *Gazetteer*, *Census Report*, *Administration Report* and in some other official documents. Their works are also a good contribution in the study of the various aspects of the socio-cultural life of the tribal people particularly of this region. But of quite long time we were not able to give a detail information about the number of research works published so far in this area of study. This work. perhaps, may be the first of its kind in this region. No doubt we may require to update the list. This will be done as a next academic programme of the Centre.

The Centre for Manipur Study is really grateful to Prof. N. Bijoy Singh, the Vice-Chancellor of Manipur University for taking leadership in the process of the revitalization of the activities of the Centre. The publication of this bibliography itself is one of the biggest contributions to the process of the improvement of the academic activities of the Centre.

I am fully convinced that this publication will certainly render contribution to those researches who are interested in the study of the life and culture of the tribal people of the region.

Prof. N. JOYKUMAR SINGH
Director
Centre for Manipur Studies

PREFACE

Tribal studies is an important academic discipline in India. Starting from the reports on the tribal communities in different parts of British India, in the form the Gazatteers, Census and Admininstrative reports ethnographic studies were carried out by the anthropologists during the colonial period. With the establishment of Anthropological Survey of India and opening of Anthropology as an academic discipline in Indian Universities there has been a tremendous growth of Tribal Studies. Many administrators, social scientists and journalist also joined on this great academic ventures.

In Manipur, reports of the Colonial Officers like, W. Mcullock, R. Brown, E.W. Dun, T.C. Hodson, John Shakespere, Willian Pettigrew, William Shaw had written volumes on the tribes of Manipur. T.C. Hodson's Naga Tribes of Manipur, Johan Shakespeare's Lushai Kuki Clan, William Shaw's Notes on Thadou Kukis are still good reference and T.C. Das's Purum (1945) is still a classic in this field.

After independence, there has been tremendous interest on the hill tribes of Manipur. The Centre for Tribal Studies of Manipur University is also generating interest in field.

In order to make this various publication by different writers on the Tribal Studies, a bibliography has been prepared jointly by the Research Scholars of the Centre. Our Purpose is to put title of the subject in single volume.

I thank the research scholars who have complied this Bibliography which may be helpful of the research scholars.

Prof. GANGMUMEI KAMEI
Co-ordinator/CTS
Manipur University
Imphal

Contents

BOOKS

Abbi, B. L. (ed.), *North East Region: Problems and Prospects of Development*. Chandigarh, Centre for Research in Rural and Industrial Development, 1981.

Acharyya, N.N., *A Brief History of Assam* (From earliest to the year 1983), Omsons Publications, Gauhati, 1987.

Acharyya, N.N., *Assam and Neighbouring States: Historical Documents*, New Delhi, Omsons Pub. 1983.

Acharyya, N.N., *North East: As Viewed by Foreigners*. New Delhi, Omsons Pub. 1985.

Acharyya, N.N., *The History of Medieval Assam*, R. Kumar, Omsons Pub., New Delhi, 1984.

Agarwal, A.K., *Economic Problems and Planning in North-East India*, 1987.

Agarwala, S.N., *India's Population Problems*, Tata McGraw Hill, New Delhi, 1975.

Agarwala, S.N., *Population*, National Book Trust, New Delhi, 1967.

Ahluwalia, B.K. and Ahluwalia, S., *Social Change in Manipur*, Cultural Publishing House, New Delhi, 1984.

Aiyappan, A., *Report on the Socio-Economic Conditions of the Aboriginal Tribes of the Province of Madras*, Govt. Printing Press, Madras, 1948.

Aiyappan, A., *Social Revolution in a Kerala Village*, Asia Publishing House, Bombay, 1965.

Aiyappan, A., *Anthropology and Tribal Welfare*, Second All India Seminar on Tribal Welfare, Bhubaneswar, 1964.

Alan, K., *Planning in North-East India*, 1985.

Alexander, W.J., *Economic Geography*, Prentice Hall of India, (P) Ltd. New Delhi-110001.

Ali, S.M., *The History of Jaintia*, Dacca, 1954.

All India Handicraft Board, *Handicrafts of Assam*, All India Handicrafts Board, New Delhi, (n.d.)

Allen, B. C., *Gazetteer of the Naga Hills and Manipur*, Shillong, 1902.

Allen, Gait, *Gazetteer of Bengal and North-East India*, Delhi, Mittal Publications.

Amalsad, D.N., *Handloom Weaving*, Orient Longmans Madras, 1961.

Ambastha, N.K. *A Critical Study of Tribal Education*, S. Chand, New Delhi,1969.

Anand, V.K., *Conflict in Nagaland, A Study of Insurgency and Counter Insurgency*, Chanakya Publications, New Delhi 1980.

Anand, V.K., *Nagaland in Transition*, Associated Publishing House, New Delhi 1967.

Anderson, J.D., *A Collection of Kachari Folk-Tales and Rhymes*, Assam Secretariat Printing Office, 1895.

Ansari, M.A., *Tribal in Criminal Web*, D.K. Publishers Distributors (P) Ltd., New Delhi..

Ansari, S.A., *Economic Geography of the Union Territory of Manipur*, D. Phil. Thesis, Gauhati, 1969.

Ansari, S.A., *Some Aspects of the Geography of Manipur*, 1985.

Archer, W.G., *Tribal Law and Justice A Report on the Santal*, D.K. Publishers Distributors (P) Ltd., New Delhi..

Army Headquarters, India, *North and North-Eastern Frontier Tribes of India* 1980 (1907), Cultural Publishing House, New Delhi.

Atkinson, E.T.H., *The Himalyan District of North Western Province of India*, N.W. & Oudh Press, Allahabad, 1884-86.

Awasty, I., *Between Sikkim and Bhutan: The Lepchas and Bhutias of Pedong*, D.K. Publisher Distributors (P) Ltd. New Delhi.

Badgaiyan, S.D., *Demographic study of Madhya Pradesh*, International Institute for Population Studies, Bombay, 1960.

Bahadur, K.P., *Caste, Tribes and Culture of India*, Assam, Ess Ess Publications, New Delhi, 1977.

Bahadur, K.P., *Population crisis in India*, National Publishing House, New Delhi, 1977.

Bailey, F.M., *No Passport of Tibet* (Discriptions of Mishimis & Monfras). London, 1957.

Bailey, F.M., *China-Tibet-Assam*, London, 1945.

Bailey, F.G., *Tribe, Caste and Nation*, Oxford University Press, Bombay, 1960.

Baines, Athelestance, *Ethnography: Castes and Tribes*, D.K. Publishers & Distributors (P) Ltd., New Delhi.

Baingley, A.H., *Jats, Gujars and Ahirs*, Government Printing Press, Calcutta, 1904.

Balakrishna, S., *Family Planning Attitude, Knowledge and Practice: A Sample Survey in Andhra Pradesh*, National Institute of Community Development, Hyderbad, 1970.

Balartnam, L.K., *Society in India*, Social Science Association, Madras, 1958.

Ball, V., *Jungle Life in India*, London, 1880.

Ball, V., *Tribal and Peasant Life in Nineteenth Century India*, Reprint, D.K. Publishers Distributors (P) Ltd., New Delhi.

Bandopadhyay, P., *Settlement Patterns of Eastern Kolhar*, 19(1), 20-26, 1957.

Bandhu, Desh and Garh, R.K., *Social Forestry and Tribal Development*. D.K. Publishers' Distributors (P) Ltd, Delhi.

Bandhyopadhyay, P.K., *Leadership Amont the Mizos: An Eurging Dimensions*, 1985.

Banerjee, A.C., *The Eastern Frontier of British India*, 1986.

Banerjee, N.K. 'An Apprisal of Shifting Cultivation in India', M.L. Patel (ed), *Agro-Economic Problems of Tribal India*. Progress Publishers, Bhopal, 1972.

Bardhan, A.B., *The Tribal Problem in India*, Communist Party Publication, New Delhi, 1973.

Bareh, H., *A Short History of Khasi Literature*, Shillong, 1969.

Bareh, Hamlet, *Khasi Democracy*, Shillong, 1963.

Bareh, Hamlet, *Khasi Fables and Folk Tales*, Calcutta, 1971.

Bareh, Hamlet, *Meghalaya*, North-Eastern India News & Feature Service, Shillong.1974.

Bareh, Hamlet, *Nagaland District Gazetteer*, Kohima, 1970.

Bareh, Hamlet, *Problems of Meghalaya.*

Bareh, Hamlet, *The History and Culture of the Khasi People*, Calcutta, 1969.

Barkataki, S., *Tribes of Assam*, National Book Trust, New Delhi, 1969.

Barkataki, S.N., *Tribal Folk Tales of Assam (Hills)*, Publication Board, Assam, Gauhati, 1970.

Barnet, *Antiquities of India*, London, 1906.

Barooah, Nirode, K., *David Scoot in Northeast India 1802-1831, A Study of British Patternalism*, Munshiram Manoharalal, (Oriental Publishers), New Delhi, 1970.

Barpujari, H.K., *Problems of the Hill Tribes North East Frontier (1899-42)*, Vol.I, II, Lawyers Book Stall, Gauhati, Assam, 1970.

Bartilli, L.J., *Soil Survey and Land Use Planning*. Soil Sci. Society. 1966.

Barua, B.K., *A Cultural History of Assam*, Vol. I. 1951.

Barua, J.K., *Idu Mishimis*, Shillong, 1961.

Barua, H., *The Red River and the Bene Hills*, 1956.

Baruah, Tapan Kumar, N., *The Singphos and Theie Religion*, Shillong,1977.

Basu, Minerdra Nath, *Tribal Art and Handicrafts*. Bharatiya Adimjati Savk Sangh, New Delhi, 1958.

Basavarajappa, K.G., *Effects of Improvement in Mortality on the Birth Rate and Related Measures*, IIPS, Bombay, 1961.

Bareja, J.D., *Accross the Golden Heights of Assam & NEFA*, Calcutta, 1961.

Baveja, J.D., *New Horizones of North East*, Western Book Depot, Gauhati, 1982.

Baveja, J.D., *The Land Where the Bamboo Flowers*. Assam Publication Board, Gauhati, 1970.

Beamls, J., *Outlines of Indian Philology: An Appendix ques Abor, Miri & Dofla Memorals*, Calcutta, 1967.

Beaujiu-Garniu, *Geography of Population*, (Second Edition) Longman Group Limited Longman Iac, New York.

Bedi, M.S., *Drinking Behaviour and Development in Tribal Areas*, D.K. Publishers Distributers (P) Ltd., New Delhi.

Bengamin, Joseph, *Scheduled Caste in Indian Politics and Society*, D.K. Publishers, New Delhi-7.

Beresford, G.W., *Notes on the North-Eastren Frontier of Assam*, Shillong, 1881.

Bernard Berelson (ed.), *Population Policy in Developed Countries*, Macgraw-Hill Book Company, New York, 1974.

Beteille, Andre, *Tribal Religion, Religious Beliefs and Practices among the Santals*, D.K. Publishers Distributors (P) Ltd., New Delhi.

Bhagbatti, Ananda and Bhowmic, P.K., *The Lodhas of West Bengal: A Socio-Economic Study*, Panthi Pustak, Calcutta, 1963.

Bhardwaj, K.S., *Demographic Study of Pharanakhorn Province*, Bombay Demographic Training and Reacher Centre, Bombay, 1955.

Bhardwaj, A.N., *Problems of Scheduled Castes and Tribes in India*, D.K. Publishers Distributors (P) Ltd. New Delhi.

Bhasin, Veena, *Ecology Culture and Change: Tribals of Sikkim Himalayas*, Inter-India Publications, New Delhi, 1989.

Bhattacharjee, Jayanta., *Cachar Under British Rule in North East India*, Radiant Publisher E-155 Kalkaji, New Delhi.

Bhattacharjee J.B. (ed.), *Sequences of Development in North East India: A Study of Tradition, Continuity and Change*, 1989.

Bhattacharjee J.B. (ed.), *Social Tension in North-East India*, 1982.

Bhattacharjee J.B. (ed.), *The Garos and the English-1765-1874*, Radiant Publishers, New Delhi.

Bhattacharjee, K.K., *North East India : A Study*, Cosmo Publications, New Delhi, 1983.

Bhat, Sudhakar, *The Challenge of the North East*, Delhi,1989.

Bhattacharjee, S.R., *Tribal Insurgency in Tripura, A Study in Exploration of Causes*, Inter-India Publications, New Delhi.

Bhattacharjee, Janmay, *Sociology of the Karbis*, D.K. Publishers Distributors (P) Ltd., New Delhi.

Bhattacharjee, T.K. *Alluring Frontier*, D.K. Publishers, New Delhi.

Bhende, Asha A. and Kanitkar, Tara, *Principles of Population Studies*, Himalaya Publishing House, Bombay, 1982.

Bhogeswar, Oinam, (ed.), *Manipuri Lokasahitya*, Unpublished Manuscript, Imphal, State Kala Academy.

Bhomwick, K.L., *Tribal India*, World Press, Calcutta, 1971.

Bhuyan, S.K., *Anglo Assamese Relation 1771-1826, A Standard Work, Describes early Policy towards the tribes*, Gauhati, 1949.

Biswas, P.C., *Santals of the Santal Pargana*, New Delhi, 1956.

Biswas, P.C., *The Santal*, Bhartiya Adimjati Sevak Sangh, New Delhi, 1966a.

Biswas, P.C., The Santal, Bhartiya Adimjati Sevak Sangh, New Delhi, 1956

Bodding, P.O., *How the Santals Live*, Institute for Sommen-lighed de Kutturforskning, Oslo, 1940.

Bodding, P.O., *Santal Folk Tales*, Harvard University Press, 1926.

Bompas, *C.H. Folklore of Santal Paraganas*, Collected by Rev. O. Bodding and Translated by C.H. Bompas, London, 1909a.

Barooah, G.L. Population Geography of Assam, K.M. Mittal Publication,B-2/19-B, Lawrence Road, M5, New Delhi.

Bose, Ashish, *Process of Urbanisation in India*: 1901-1951, Univers of Delhi (Ph.D. Thesis), 1959.

Ashish, Bose, et. al (ed), *Studies in Demography*, George Allen and Unwin Ltd. London, 1970.

Bose, J.K., *Glimpses of Tribal Life in North-East India*, Institute of Social Research and Applied Anthropology, Calcutta, 1980.

Bose Manilal, *British Policy in the North-East Frontier Agency.*

Bose Manilal, *Historical and Constitutional Documents of North-Eastern India*, 1824-1973.

Bose, N.K., Tribal Life in India, 1971, New Delhi.

Bose, P.K., *Classes and Class Relation among Tribals of Bengal*, Ajanta Publishers, New Delhi, D. K. Publishers Distributors (p) Ltd., New Delhi.

Bower, U.G., *Naga Path*, Adventure to Naga Inhabited Areas, John Murray, London.

Bower, Ursulla Graham, *The Hidden Land*, Allied Publishers Private Ltd. 15 J.N. Herdio-Marg Ballard Estate, Bombay.

Bradley, Birt, F.B., *Chotanagpur:A Little Known Province of the Empire*, Smith Elders & Co., London, 1903.

Breeks, James Willkinson, *Primitive Tribes & Monuments of the Nilgiris*, New Delhi,1983.

Briggs, W.G. *The Chamars*, Association Press Calcutta, 1920.

Brinkman R, and Syonth A.J., *Land Evaluation for Rural Purposes*, Pune 17, Intera, Inst. Land Reclan and Improvement (ILRI) 1973.

Brown R., *Statiscal Account of Manipur*, Calcutta, 1874.

Buchanan, D.H., *Eastern India*, Calcutta, 1934.

Burlings, Robbins, *Renganggri*, University of Pennsyalvania Press, Philadelphia, 1963.

Burrard, S.G., *Records of Survey of India, Exploitation on the North-East Frontier during 1911-12-13*, Calcutta, 1914.

Buttler, John., A sketch of Assam, with some Account of the Hill Tribes,by an officer, London, 1847.

Butta, J., *Travels and Adventures in the Province of Assam during a Residence of Fourteen Years*, Smith Elder and Co., London, 1855.

Campbell, Arthur, *The Seize*, George Allen & Unwin Ltd. Ruskin House Museum Street London, 1957 (4th Impression).

Campbell, Arthur, *Santal Folktales*, Santhal Mission Press, Pukhuria, Bengal, 1891.

Carawley, Earnesty, *Dimensions of Marriage in Primitive society*, 2 Volms. 1989 TriPathi Book Service. New Delhi.

Carey, S. & H. N. Luck, The Chin Hills, Vol. I & II Cultural Publishing House, Delhi.

Carnegy, P. T. *Tour Diaries of the Deputy Commissioner Naga Hills*, 1876-7. Continued by W. J.Williamson & G. H. Damant Shillong, 1942.

Carnegy, R., *Report on the Administration of Naga Hills*, Calcutta, 1877.

Carrapiett, W. J. S., *The Kachin Tribes of Burma*, 1929 Rangoon.

Census of India, Census of India 1981 Series-I . India, part II-B (iii)Primary Census, Abstract, Scheduled Tribes.

Chaki-Sirkar, Manjusri, *Feminism in a Traditional Society Shakti Books*, Delhi,1984.

Chakladu, S., *Minority Rights:A Sociolinguistic Analysis of group Conflicts in Eastern Region of India*, 1987.

Chakrabarti S. B., Social Science and Social Concern (Felicitation Volume in Honour of Prof. B. K. Roy Burman). D. K. Publishers Distributors (p) Ltd., New Delhi.

Chakraberty, Chandra, *Prehistory of India*, Calcutta, 1948.

Chakraborti, M & D. Mukherji, *Indian Tribes*, Seraswat Library Calcutta-6, 1971.

Chakravorty, B. C. *British Relations With the Hill Tribes of Assam since 1858*, Calcutta, 1964.

Chakravarti, Nalini Ranjan, *The Indian Minority in Burma*, Oxford University Press, London, 1971.

Chakravarti, R., *People of Manipur*, 1986.

Challiana, Pastor., *Pi Pu Nun*, ("The Ancestor's way of Life"), The Trio Book House, Aizwal, 1971.

Chandra, R. C. and Sidhu M. S. *Introduction to Population Geography*, Kalyani Publisher, New Delhi, 1980.

Chandrashekhran, S., *Infant Mortality in India 1901-1955*, Allen and Unwin, London, 1959.

Chandrashekhran, S., *Demography and the Statistician Demographyic Problems of Eastran India*, Bureau of Applied Economics and Statistics, Calcutta, 1960.

Chang, Imlong, *A Guide Book in Chang Naga Dialect or Anglo-Chang* (Makokchung) ,1956.

Chapekar, L. N., *The Thakurs of Sahadri*. Oxford University Press, Bombay, 1960.

Chapmann, R. A. B., *Political Agents Notes*, 1898, Unpublished Jagdalpur Records Room.

Chanbisa, M. L., *Caste Tribe and Exploitation Exploration of Inegualit at Village Leval*, D. K. Publishers Distributors (p) Ltd., New Delhi.

Chaudhuri, A. B., *The Santals, Religion and Rituals* D. K. Publishers Distributors (p) Ltd., New Delhi.

Chaudhuri, A.B., *Witchkilling Amonmgst Santhals*. K.K. Publishers Distributors (P) Ltd., New Delhi.

Chaudhuri, Buddhadev (ed), *Tribal Health, Socio-Cultural Dimensions*, D. K. Publishers Distributors (p) Ltd., New Delhi.

Chaudhuri, Buddhadev (ed), *Tribal Development in India, Inter-India Publications*, New Delhi, 1982.

Chaudhuri, T.K., Demographic Trends in Assam, B. R. Publishing corporation, Delhi,1982.

Chase, H.C., *The Relationship of Certain Biological and Social-Economic Factors to Foetal Infant and Early Childhood Mortality*, State Dept. of Health, Albany, New York, 1962.

Chatterji, A. and T. C. Das, *The Hos of Seraikella*, Calcutta, 1972.

Chatterjee, S.K., Kirata Jana Kirti, the Indo-Mongoloids, their contributions to the history and culture of India.

Chatterjee, S.P., Land Utilization in the District of 24- Parganas, Bengal, 1948. Calcutta.

Chaube, S. *Hill Politics in North- East India*, Orient Longman, N. Delhi, 1973.

Chawla, D.R., *Need for a Population Commission*, New Era Publication, Simla, 1962.

Chib Sukhdev Singh, This Beautiful India Meghalaya, Light and Life Publishers, New Delhi.

Chib Sukhdev Singh, *Caste Tribes and Culture of India* Vol. 9 Andaman Nicobar & Lakshadeep Islands, D.K. Publishers Distributors (P) Ltd., New Delhi.

Choudhouri, R., *Some Historical Aspects of Feudalism in Ancient India*, Trivandrum 1959.

Choudhury, P. C., *The History of Civilization of People of Assam to the* 5th Century A. D., Gauhati, 1959.

Choudhury, B. N., *Some Cultural and Linguistic Aspects of the GAROS*, LAWYERS BOOK STALL, GAUHATI, 1969.

Choudhury, J. N., *Arunachal through the Ages* (From Frontier Tract to Union Territory Published by Smt. Jaya Chowdhury Shillong.

Clark, (Mrs), M. M. *A Corner of India*, Philadelphia, 1907.

Clark (Mrs) B. W., *An Ao Naga Grammer*;Chongli Dialect of Naga, 1893. Shillong

Clark (Mrs) B. W., *Ao Naga Dictionary*, Calcutta, 1911.

Clerk, C., *Population Growth and Laod Use*, Mac-Millan, London. 1967.

Coale, AJ & E. M. *Population Growth and Economic Development in Low-Income Countries, Princeton*, New Jersey, 1958.

Codrington, K. De. B., The Raj Gonds of Adilabad, Mac-Millan Co., London, 1945.

Constatine, R., Manipur, *Maid of the Mountains*, New Delhi, Lancers Pub.1981.

Cooper, T.T. *The Mishmee Hills, Henrys King* & Co., London, 1873, Reprinted by Wen Publishing Co. 1971.

Crooke, W., *The Tribes and Castes of the North Western Provinces and Oudh*, Calcutta, 1896a, 4 Vols.

Crooke, W., *The Tribes and Castes of the North Western India*, Cosmo Publication, Delhi-6, 1974.

Crooke, W., *Races of Northern India*, Cosmo Publications, Delhi-6, 1973.

Crooke, W., *Natives of Northern India*, Cosmo Publications, Delhi-35. 1980.

Culshaw, W.J., *Tribal Heritage* (the Santhal), London, 1949.

Danda, Dipali G., *Among the Dimasa of Assam* (Kachari Tribe): An Ethnographic Study Sterling Publishers Pvt. Ltd., New Delhi, 1978.

Dandekar, Kumudini, *Demographic Survey of Six Rural Communities*, Asia Publishing House, Bombay, 1959.

Dandekar, V.M. & Kummud ni Dandekar, *Survey of Fertility and Mentality in Poona District,* Gokhle Institute of Politics and Economics, Poona Publication No. 27, 1953.

Das, A.K., *Tribal Art and Craft*, 1939b, Agam Kala Prakashan, New Delhi.

Das, A.K., *The Koras and Soma Little known community of West Bengal*, Cultural Research institute, Govt. of West Bengal, Calcutta, 1964.

Das, A.K., *The Totos*, Cultural Research Institute Government of West Bengal, Calcutta, 1969.

Das, A.K. and Banerjee, H.N., *The Impact of Tea Industry on the Life of the Tribals of West Bengal* Cultural Research Institute, Govt. of West Bengal, Calcutta, 1964b.

Das, A.K. and Banerjee, S.K., *The Lepcha of Darjeeling District Cultural Research Institute, Govt. of West Bengal*, Calcutta, 1962b.

Das, A.K. and Banerjee, S.K., *Impact of Industrialization on the Life of the Tribals of West Bengal*, Cultural Research Institute, Govt. of West Bengal, Cal. 1962a.

Das A.K. & Raha M.K., *The Oraons of Sunderban*, Cultural Research Institute, Govt. of West Bengal, Calcutta, 1963.

Das A.K. Raha, M.K. & Roy Choudhury B.K., *The Malpaharians of West Bengal* Cultural Research Institute, Govt. of West Bengal, Cal. 1966a.

Das A.K. & Raha, M.K., *West Bengal Tribes Through Photographs*, Cultural Research Institute, Govt. of West Bengal, Calcutta, 1965.

Das, A.K., Raha, M.K. and and Roy Choudhary, B.K., *Handbook on Scheduled Castes and Tribes of West Bengal*, Cultural Research Institute, govt. of West Bengal, Calcutta, 1966b.

Das, A.M., *Impact of Tea Industry on the Life of Tribes of West Bengal*, Government of West Bengal, Calcutta, 1949.

Das, B.M., Ethnic Affinities of Radha, Gauhati, 1960.

Das, Gupta, A. *et. al.*, *Couple Fertility*, National Sample Survey, Delhi, Govt. of India Paper 7 (Undated).

Dasgupta, N.K. *Problems of Tribal Education and the Santals*, Bharatiya Adimjati Sevak Sangh, New Delhi, 1964.

Dasgupta, P.K., *Life and Culture of Matrilineal Trible of Meghalaya*,1984.

Das K.N., Population and Land use Changes in the Kosi Region Bihar, Ph.D. Thesis Bhagalpur University, 1969.

Das N.K., *Ethnic Identity, Ethnicity and Social Stratification in North* East India, (Inter India Publications) Delhi, 1989.

Das R. K. *Tribal Social Structure: A Study of the Maring Society of Manipur* 1989.

Das S.L. *Pattern of Population and Land Use in the District of Bhagalpur*, ph. D. Thesis, Bhagalpur University, 1979.

Das, Tarakchandra, *The Purums: An Old kuki Tribe of Manipur*, Culcatta, 1945.

Das S.T. Tribal Life of North Eastern India, Cosmo Publication, Delhi, 1973.

Dalton, E.T., *Tribal History of Eastern India* Cosmo Publication, Delhi, 1973.

Dalton, E.T., *Descriptive Ethnology of Bengal.* Government Printing Press, Calcutta, 1872.

Datta Ray, B., *Social and Economic Profile of North-East India*, 1978.

Datta Ray, B., *Assam Secretariat 1874-1947, An Administrative History of North East India.*

Datta Ray, B., Tribal Identity and Tension in North East India. 1989.

Datta Ray, B., *The Pattern and Problems of Population in North East India*, 1987.

Datta Ray, B., *North East India 2000 A.D.* 1987.

Davis K., *Population of India and Pakistan New Jersey*, 1951.

Dawan Singh, Rongmuthu, *Folk Tales of the Garos*, Calcutta, 1960.

Dena Lal., *Christian Missions and Colonialism, Vendrame Insitute*, Shillong, 1988.

Dena Lal., *British Policy Towards Manipur* 1891-1919, Imphal, 1984.

Deogaonkar, S.G., *Presiems of Development of Tribal Areas*, Leeladevi Publications, Delhi, 1980.

Desai, P.B., A Survey of Research in Demography, Popular Prakashan, Bombay, 1975.

Dev, Bimal and Dilip K. Lahiri, Manipur Culture and Politics, Mittal Publications, New Delhi, 1987.

Devi (Mrs.) Lakshimi, *Ahom Tribal Relations (A Political Study)*, The Authress, Cotton College, Gauhati, 1968.

Dickenson, J.P., *A Geography of the Third World*, Methuen and Co. in association with Methuen, Inc. 733 Third Avenue, New York.

Deshpande, M.M., *Aryan and Non Aryan in India*, Ann Arbar, 1979.

Deshpande, V., *Adivasis of Thane*, D.K. Publishers Distributors, Delhi.

Dev, Bimal and Lahiri, *Lushai Customs and Ceremonies.*

Dev, S.C., *Nagaland, the Untold Story*, Calcutta, 1988.

Dhan, R.O., These are my Tribesmen: the Oraon, Ranchi, 1967.

Dhasmona, M.M., The Ramos of Arunachal, A Socio-Cultural Study, D.K. Publishers Distributers (P) Ltd. Delhi.

Dihingia, Hemeswar, *Assams Struggles Against British Rule 1826-1863*, K.D. Bhatia for Asian Publication Services, New Delhi.

Dobbort, Marion Lundy, *Ethnographic Research*, Praeger, New York, 1982.

Dongali, John Mac, *Land of Religion, The Sardar and Kherwar Monuments in Bihar 1858-95*, D.K. Publishers Distributors (P) Ltd., New Delhi.

Doshi, S.L., Processes of Tribal Unification and Integration, D.K. Publishers Distributors (P) Ltd., New Delhi..

Doshi, S.L., Bhils Between Societel Self Awareness and Cultural Systhesis, 1971.

Doshi, S.L., Progresses of Tribal Unification and Integration, Council Publishing, Company, New Delhi, 1978.

Downs, Fredrick, S. *Christianity in North East India, ISPCK*, New Delhi, 1983.

Driver, Edwin, *Differential Feutility in Central India*, Princeton Univ. Press New Jersey, 1963.

Dube, B.K. & Bahadur, F., *A Study of the Tribal People and Tribal Areas of Madhya Pradesh* Govt. Regional Press, Indore, 1967.

Dube, Leela, *The Gond Women* (Ph. D. Thesis, Univ. of Nagpur, Nagpur, Unpub.)

Dube, Leela, *Matriliny and Islam*, National Publishing House, Delhi, 1969.

Dube, S.C., *The Kamar*, Lucknow, 1951.

Dube, S.C., Tribal Heritage of India, Vikas Publishing House, New Delhi, 1977.

Dube, S.N. & Murdia, Ratna, *Land Alienation and Restoration in Tribal Communities in India*, D.K. Publishers Distributors (P) Ltd., New Delhi..

Dube K.C., *The Hill Marias of Bastar*, Bhopal, Vol.I, 1983, (Unpub. Ph. D. Thesis).

Dun, E.W., *Gazetteer of Manipur*, Delhi, Vivek Pub. House 1975 (Rep).

Duyker, Edward, *Tribal Guerillas, The Santals of West Bengal and the Naxalite* Movement. D. K. Publishers Distributors (P) Ltd. New Delhi.

Dutta, B.B. & Karna M.N. (eds). *Land Relations in North East India*, 1987.

Dutta, M.P. *The People of NEFA, The Tangsas of Namchik and Tribal Village*, Shillong, 1959.

Dutta, Majumdar, N., *The Senthal, A Study in Culture Change*, Manager of Publications, Govt. of India Press, Calcutta, 1956.

Dutta, Promatha Nath, Impact of the West on the Khasis and Jaintias *(A Survey of Political, Economic and Social Changes)* Cosmo Publications, New Delhi,1982.

Dutta, Shosee Chunder, *The Wild Tribes of India*, Cosmo Publications, New Delhi, 1984.

Ehrenfels, U.R., *Kadar of Cochin*, University of Madras, Madras, 1952.

Elliot, H., *Memoris on the History, Folklore & Distribution of the Races in N.W.P.* Being and amplified edition, 1868.

Elwin, Varrier (ed). *A New Deal for Tribal India*, Ministry of Home Affairs, New Delhi, 1963.

Elwin, Varrier (ed). '*The Aborigenals*'Oxford Pamphlets of Indian Affairs, Bombay, 1943, 2nd ed. 1944.

Elwin, Varrier (ed). A Philosophy of NEFA, The Advisor to Government of Assam, Shillong, 1960.

Elwin, Varrier (ed). *Bondo Highlanders*, Oxford University Press, Bombay, 1950.

Elwin, Varrier (ed). *Phulmah of the Hills: A Tale of the Gonds*, John Murray, London, 1937.

Elwin, Varrier (ed). Demography of NEFA, NEFA Administration, Shillong, 1965.

Elwin Verrier(ed.) ., Indian North-East Frontier in the Nineteenth Century, Oxford House.

Elwin, Varrier (ed). *Marica Murder and Suicide*, Oxford University Press, Bombay, 1942a.

Elwin, Varrier (ed). *Folktales of Mahakoshal*, Oxford Univ. Press, London, 1944.

Elwin, Varrier, *Mythys of Middle India*, Oxford University Press, London, 1947b.

Elwin, V. & Hiwale S., *Folksongs of the Maikal Hills*, Humphe Milford, Bombay, 1944.

Elwin, V. & Hiwale S., *Songs of Forest*, George Allen & Unwin, London, 1935a& b.

Elwin, Verrier, *The Aboriginal*, Oxford Univ. Press, London, 1943.

Elwin, Verrier, *The Art of NEFA*, NEFA Administration, Shillong, 1963.

Elwin, Verrier, *The Baiga*, John Murrey, London, 1939.

Elwin, Varrier, *The Art of the Northeast Frontier of India*, NEFA, Shillong, 1959.

Elwin, Varrier, *The Muria and Their Ghotul*, Oxford Univ. Press, London, 1947a.

Elwin, Verrier, *The Myths of North-East Frontier of India*, NEFA, Shillong, 1958.

Elwin, Varrier, *The Nagas in the Nineteenth Century*, Oxford Univ. Press, Ely House, London W. i. (India) Oxford House, Appllo Bunder, Bombay IBR, 1969.

Elwin, Varrier, *The Religion of Indian Tribe*, (The Saora), London, 1954.

Elwin, Varrier, The Tribal Art of Middle India, Oxford Univ. Press, London, 1983.

Elwin, Varrier, *The Tribal World of Verrier*, Elwin Oxford Univ. Press, London, 1964.

Endle, S. *The Kacharis*, MacMillan and Co., London, 1961.

Emkey, Steplen, *Economics for Development*, Devis Hobson, London, 1961.

Enthoven, R.E., *Tribes and Castes of Bombay*, (3 Vols.) Government Central Press, Bombay, 1920-22.

Evan, Pritchard, E.E., *The Muer*, Oxford, 1940.

Ferriera, J.V., *Totemism in India*, Oxford University Press, Bombay, 1965.

Firth, R.W., *Social Change in Tikopia*, Allen & Unwin, London, 1958.

Foning, A.R. Lepcha, My Vanishing Tribe, Sterling Publishers Private Ltd., New Delhi, 1958.

Fuchs, S., *The Gond and Bhumia of Eastern Mandla*, Asia Publishing House, Bombay, 1960.

Furnes, W.H., *The Ethnography of the Nagas in East Assam*.

Furer-Haimendrof Christoph Von, *The Gonds of Andhra Pradesh*, London George Allen & Unwin, 1979.

Furer-Haimendrof Christoph Von, (ed.), *Asian Highland Societies: An Anthropological Puspective*.

Furer-Haimendrof Fhristoph Von, (ed.), *Ethnographic Notes on the Tribes of the Subansiri Region*, Shillong, India, 1947.

Furer-Haimendrof Fhristoph Von, (ed.), *Exploration in the Eastern Himalayas Assam Government Press*, Shillong, 1947.

Furer-Haimendrof Fhristoph Von, (ed.), *Highlanders of Arunchal Pradesh: Anthropological Research in North-East India*, Vikash Publishing House Pvt. Ltd. Red. Office: 5 Ansari Road, New Delhi, 1982.

Furer-Haimendrof Fhristoph Von, (ed.), *Himalayan Adventure Early Travels in North East India*, Published by S.K. Ghai Sterling Managing Director L-10, Green Park Extension, New Delhi.

Furer-Haimendrof Fhristoph Von, (ed.), *Himalayan Barbary*, John Murray, London, 1955.

Furer-Haimendrof Fhristoph Von, (ed.), *Religion and Ethics Among the Konyak Nagas and Other Indian Tribes*, Essays in Anthropology Presented to Rai Bahadur, S.C. Roy, pp. 15868.

Furer-Haimendrof Fhristoph, C. Von, *The Naked Nagas*, London, 1939. Calcutta, Thakur Spink & Co. Pvt. Ltd. 1933.

Furer-Haimendrof Fhristoph, C. Von., *Return to the Naked Nagas.*

Furer-Haimendrof Fhristoph, C. Von., *The Apa Tanis and Their Neighbours: A Primitive Civilization of the Eastern Himalayas*, Routledge and Kegan Paul, London, 1962.

Furer-Haimendrof Fhristoph, C. Von., *The Konyak Nagas*, Holt, Rinchart & Winston, New York, 1969.

Furer-Haimendrof Fhristoph, C. Von., *The Chenchus : Jungle Folk of Deccan*, MacMillan & Co. London, 1943.

Furer-Haimendrof Fhristoph, C. Von., The Raj Gonds of Adilabad: A Peasant Culture of Deccan, MacMillan & Co. London, 1948.

Furer-Haimendrof Fhristoph, C. Von., *The Reddis of Biron Hills : A Study in Accul-turation*, 2 vols., Mac- Millan & Co. London, 1945b.

Furer-Haimendrof Fhristoph, C. Von., *The Tribal Population of Hyderbad*, Hyderbad Revenue Department, Hyderbad, 1945a.

Furer-Haimendrof Fhristoph, C. Von., *Tribes of India*, Oxford University Press, Delhi, 1982.

Furer-Haimendrof Fhristoph, C. Von., *Tribes of India : The Struggle for Survival.*

Gait, E. A., *A History of Assam*, Cal & Simla, 1926.

Ganguli, B. N., *Population and Development*, S. Chand & Co.(Pvt.) Ltd. New Delhi, 1973.

Ganguli, M., *House Building in the Villages of the Maram Naga Tribe*, New Orient, 1966.

Gassah, L.S., *Garo Hills Land the People*, Omsons Publications, Gauhati,1984.

Geoffery,E & Antony, B. J., *Imphal*, New York, Macmillan & Co. Ltd.

German, G. P., *Report of the United Khasi-Jaintia*

Autonomous District Commission on the matter of creation of a new Autonomous District for the Jewai Sub Division., Shillong, 1964.

Geisburg N., *The Regional Concept and Planning in Asia and Far East*, Chicago, 1975.

Ghurye, G.S., *The aborigines So-called and Their Future*, Gokhale Institute of Politics and Economics, Poona, 1943.

Ghurye, G.S., *Mahadeo Kolis*, Popular Book Depot,1957.

Ghurye, G.S., *The Scheduled Tribes*, Popular Book Depot., Bombay,1959.

Gilhodes, C., *The Kaihins: Religion and Customs*, Calcutta, 1922.

Gluckman, Max., *Order and Rebellion in Tribal Africa*, The Free Press of Glenocoe, New York, 1963.

Godden, Gertunede, M., *A Naga and Frontier Tribe of N.E.* vol. XXXII, 1902.

Godwin, A.H.K., *On the stone Mounments of the Khasi Hills Tribes and on some Peculiar Rites and customs of the People Anthropology Institute*, Vol. I, 1872.

Gogoi, Lila, *The Tai Khamtis*, Chowkhamoon Gohain (Namsoom), Ex-M.P. Chowkhan, NEFA, 1971.

Gore, F.S.T.J., *Lights & Hades of Hill Life*, Oriental Publishers, Delhi, 1972.

Gorgr, G., *Himalayan Village* : An Account of the *Lepchas of Sikkim*, Michael Joseph,London, 1938.

Gori, Gulab Khan, *Changing Phase of Tribal Area of Manipur*, B.R. Publishing Corporation, New Delhi, 1984

Goswami, B.B., *The Mizo Unrest-A Study of Politicisation of Culture*, Aalekh Publisher, Jaipur, 1979.

Goswami, P.C., *Problem of Jhum Control*, T. Mathew (ed.) Tribal Economy of North-Eastern Regions, Spectrum Publication, Gauhati, India, 1990.

Goswami, P.C. (ed.), *Socio-Economic Research in Tribal Areas* : Agro-Economic Research Centre for North Eastern India, Jorhat, 1972.

Goswani, Praphulla-datta, *Essays on the Folklore and Culture of North-Eastern India*, Spectrum Publication, Gauhati, Assam, 1983.

Gougin, T., History of Zomi, 1984 Zomi Press, Zion Street, Churachandpur, Manipur.

Government of Bihar, *Bihar Tribal Sub-Plan (1985-90)*, October, 1985.

Government of India, *Report of the Working Group on Development of Scheduled Tribes During Seventh Plan (1985-90)*, Ministry of Home Affairs, New Delhi, 1984.

Government of India, *Report on the Special Multipurpose Tribal Blocks*, Ministry of Home Affairs, New Delhi, 1960.

Government of India, *Report of the Working Group on Tribal Development During Sixth Plan, 1980-85*, Ministry of Home Affairs, New Delhi, 1980.

Government of India, *Report on the Industries and Allied Sectors in Tribal Areas*, Ministry of Home Affairs, New Delhi, 1978.

Government of India, *Census of India, 1971, Series – I* paper one of 1975, Scheduled Castes and Scheduled Tribes.

Government of India, *Census of India 1971, Series-12 Manipur Part-II-C. Social & Cultural Tables and Part V-A. Special Table for Scheduled Tribes and Castes.*

Government of India, *Census of India 1961, Vol. I, India Part V-A (ii) Special Table for Scheduled Tribes.*

Government of India, *Census of India 1961, Housing & Establishment Tables, Manipur, Part-III. Report on Housing: Part V, Tables on Scheduled Castes & Scheduled Tribes.*

Government of India, *Report of the Scheduled Areas & Scheduled Tribes Commission, Vol. I 1960-61.* Ministry of Home Affairs.

Government of India, *Report of the Study Team on Tribal Development Programme Committee on Plan Project 1969.* Planning Commission.

Government of Manipur, *Draft Sixth Five Year Plan 1980-85, Annual Plans 1981-82 Under Tribal Sub-Plan*, State Planning Department.

Government of Manipur, *Directory of Small Scale Industries*, Department of Industry, 1984.

Government of Manipur, *Annual Administration Report Hill Areas of Manipur*, Directorate of Information & Public Relations, 1980

Government of Manipur, *Annual Administration Report 1966-67, 67-78, Directorate of Information* & Public Relations.

Government of Manipur, *Statistical Handbook*, Directorate of Economic and Statistics.

Government of Manipur, *Techno-Economic Survey of Manipur 1961*, Manipur Administration, NCAER.

Guha Roy, S., *Fertility Performance and Female Age at Marriage: A Study of the Bivariate Relationship*, Indian Statistical Institute, Calcutta (MIMEOGRAPHED), 1968.

Gupta, P.B., *Demographic Report of West Bengal 1960-61*. Indian Statistical Institute, Calcutta, 1968.

Gupta, R.B., *Levels and Trends of Fertility in Bihar (1970-71)*, Demographic Research Centre, Miniographed Service No. 50. Department of Statistics, Patna Univesity, Patna, 1974.

Gurdon, P. R. T., *The Khasis*, MacMillan & Co., London, 1914.

Gurdon, P. R. T., *The Khasis*, 1981 (1907) Cosmo Publications India, New Delhi-2

Haimendrof, CVF, *Tribal Hyderabad: Four Reports*, Revenue Department, Government of H.E. H., The Nizams, Hyderbad, 1945.

Haimendrof, CFV, *Raj Gonds of Adilabad*, MacMillan Co. London, 1948.

Haimendorf F. C. Von., *Ethnographic Notes on the Tribes of* Subansire Region, Shillong, 1947.

Hamilton, A., *In Abor Jungles of North-East India*, Mittal Publications, New Delhi-35, 1983.

Hammerton, J. A., Tribes, Races & Culture of India and Neighbouring Countries Afghanistan, Bhutan, Burma, Ceylon, Srilanka, Nepal & Tibet, D. K. Publishers Distributors (P) Ltd. New Delhi.

Hammeherton, J. A. (ed.) *An Encyclopaedia of Human Races All Over the World (in 7 Vols.) Vol-I*, Gain Publishing House, Delhi, 1984.

Hammpy, S. P. *Sketch of Sing-phos*, Calcutta, 1840.

Hanson, O.A., *A Grammer of the Kachin Language*, Rangoon, 1886.

Hanson, O.A., *The Kachins:Their Customs and Traditions*, Rangoon, 1913.

Harcourt, A.F.P., *The Himalayan Districts of Kulu, Lahaul & Spiti, William A. Hallen*. London, 1871.

Hardiman, David, *The Coming of the Devi: Adivasi Assertion in Westren India*, D. K. Publishers Distributors, (P) Ltd., New Delhi.

Harkness, A., *Description of Singular Aboriginal Race, Inhabiting the Summit of the Nilgiri Mountain of Coimbatore in the Southern Peninsular of India*, Smith Elder & Co. London, 1832.

Hasan Amir, M., *Meet the U. P. Tribes*, D. K. Publishers, New Delhi.

Hasan, Amir and Seemin Hasan, *Folktales of Uttar Pradesh Tribes*, The Academic Press, Haryana, 1982.

Hasan, Amir, *The Buxas Of the Tarai: A Study of their socio-economic Disintegration. D.K. Publishers Distributors* (P) Ltd. New Delhi-7.

Hasan, Amir, *A Tribe in Tumoil: A Socio-Economic Study of Jumm Gujars of Uttar Pradesh*, D. K. Publishers , New Delhi.

Hasanin, N., Bonded for ever: *A Study of the Kolta Acis Himalayan Tribe*, D. K. Publishers Distributors (P) Ltd., New Delhi.

Hasan, Amir, *Tribal Administration in India*, D.K. New Delhi,

Hasnain, Nadeem, *Tribal India Today*, Harnam Publications, New Delhi, 1983.

Hasnain, Nadeem, *Hill Tracts Between Assam and Burma* (Selection on Paper) Pub. By Mrs. Sunan Lata, for vivek publishing Company, 18-D Kamla Nagar, New Delhi-97.

Hiralal & Russel, *Tribes and Castes of Central Provinces of India, Macmillan* & Co., London, 1916.

Hislop, Stephen, *Aboriginal Tribes of Central Provinces*, Nagpur, 1972.

Hivale, S., *The Pardhans*, Oxford, 1946.

Hockings, Paul (ed.) *Principles of Visual Anthropology*, Mouton Publishers, Paris, 1975.

Hodson, T.C., *The Meitheis*, Delhi, B.R. Pub. Corporation, 1975, (Rep.).

Hodson, T.C., *The Naga Tribes of Manipur*, Neeraj Publishing House, Delhi-52, (1911) 1984.

Hodson, T.C., *The Primitive Culture of India*, Royal Asiatic Society, James G. Forlong Fund, Vol. I London, 1922.

Hoffmann, J., *Encyclopaedia Mundarica* & Govt. Printing Press, Patna, 1950.

Horam, M., *Social and cultural Life of Nagas*, B.R. Publishing Corporation, Delhi-52, 1939b. 1977.

Horam, M., *The Naga Polity*.

Horam, M., *Nagas Old Ways and New Trends*, Cosmo Publications, New Delhi-2, 1988.

Horam, M., *Nagas Insurgency*, 1988.

Hunter, W.W., *A Statistical Account of Assam* (in two Vols.) 1st Pub. 1879, B.R. Publishing Corporation, 461, Vivekanand Nagar, Delhi-110052, 1982.

Husain, M., *Nagaland: Habitat, Society and Shifting Cultivation*, 1989.

Husain, I.Z., *Population Analysis and Studies, Bombay*, 1972.

Hutchinson, R.H. Sneyed., *Chittagong Hill Tracts*, Vivek Publishing Company, Delhi, 1978.

Hutton, J.H., *Census of India 1931 with complete Survey of Tribal* Life and System.

Hutton, J.H., *Change Language: Grammer and Vocabulary of the Language of the Chang Nagas.*

Hutton, J.H., *Report on Naga Hills.*

Hutton, J.H., *The Angami Nagas*, Oxford Univ. Press, Bombay. 1969 (Reprint).

Hutton, J.H., *The Angami Nagas with some Notes on the Neigbouring Tribes*, Macmillan & Co. London, 1921a.

Hutton, J.H., *The Sema Nagas*, Oxford University Press Ely House, London W.I. 1968 (1921a).

Ibbetson, D. *A Glowwary of the Tribes and Castes of Punjab and North West Frontier Province*, 3 Vols., Superintendent, Government Press, Punjab, Lahore, 1919.

Isaacs, Harold R., *Idols of the Tribe*, Harper & Row, Publishers London, 1817.

Iyer, L.K. and Krishna, Ananta, *Cochin Tribes and Castes*, Vol. I, II Higgan Bottan & Co., London, 1908, 1912.

Iyer, L.K. Ananta Krishna, *Lectures on Ethnography*, University of Calcutta, Calcutta, 1925.

Iyer, L.K. Ananta Krishna, *The Anthropology of Syrains Christians*, Cochin Government Press, Erona Kulan, 1926.

Iyer, L.A.K. & L.K., Balaratnam, *The Cooro Tribes and Castes*, Gurdon Press, Madras, 1948.

Iyer, L.K. Ananta Krishna, *The Mysore Tribes and Castes*, Mysore University, Mysore, 1930.

Iyer, L.K. Ananta Krishna, *The Mysore Tribes and Castes*, Vol. I, Mysore University, Mysore, 1935.

Iyer, L.K. Ananta Krishna, *The Mysore Tribes and Castes*, Vol. II Mysore University, Mysore, 1938.

Iyer, L.A. Krishna, *The Travancore Tribes & Castes*, Vol. I, II and III, Government press, Trivandrum, 1937.

Izshowity, K.G., *The Gotra Ceremony of Boro Gadaba* (ed.).

The Jadonang Death Anneversary Publication, *Jodonang, A Freedom Fighter of Manipur.*

Jay, E.J., *A Tribal Village of Middle India*, Anthropological Survey of India, Calcutta, 1970.

Jenkins, W.M., *Life and Work of Khasi Carnaroom*, 1906.

Jha, B.N., *Problems of Land Utilization*, Calsssical Publications, New Delhi.

Jha, J.C., *The Kol Insurraction in Chotanagpur*, Chacker, Spink and Co. Calcutta, 1964.

Jha, V.D., *Megalithic Monuments in Bastar*, Prachya Pratibha, 1977, V.1.

Jha, Makhan, *Reading in Tribal Culture: A Study of the Ollar of Orissa*, D.K. publishers, New Delhi.

Jha, S.D., *Arunachal Pradesh : Rich Land & Poor People*, D.K. Publishers, New Delhi.

Johri, S.N., *Our Borderlands*, Himalaya Publications, Lucknow, 1964.

Jones, H.R., *A Population Geography*, Harper & Row Publish, London.

Johnstone, James, *Manipur and the Naga Hills*, Cultural Publication House, New Delhi, 1983 (Rep.).

Johnstone, J. Sir, *Captain Welsh's Expedition to Assam* 1792-94 London, 1912.

Joshi, R., *Tribals: Islands of Deprivation*, D.K. Publishers Distributors (P) Ltd., New Delhi..

Joshi L.D., *Tribal People of the Himalayas, A Study of The Khasas*, K.M. Mittal, Mittal Publications, New Delhi, 1984.

Joshi, L.D., *The Khasa Family Law in Himalayan Districts of the United Provinces of Indian*. Government Press, Allahabad. 1929.

Kabra, G.D., *Tribal Workers in an Industrial Setting*, D.K. Publishing Distributers (P) Ltd., New Delhi.

Kabra, K.N., *Dependence and Dominance Political Economy of a Tribal Community*, D.K. Publishers Distributors (P) Ltd., New Delhi..

Kabui, Gangmumei, *Anal : A Transborder Tribe of Manipur*, Mittal Publications, Delhi, 1985.

Kabui, Gangmumei, *The Koirengs of Manipur*, Koren Youth Organisation, Imphal, 1986.

Kabui, Gangmumei (ed), *Tribal Profile of Manipur*, Centre for Tribal Studies, Manipur University, Canchipur, 1988.

Kamkhenthang, H. *The Paite : A Transborder Tribe of India and Burma*, D.K. Publishers Distributors, P Ltd., New Delhi.

Kar, Parimal Chandra, *British Annexation of Garo Hills*, Naba-Bharat Publishers, 72 Mahatma Gandhi Road, Cal-9, 1970.

Kar, Parimal Chandra, *The Garos in Transition*, Cosmo Publications, New Delhi, 1982.

Karotemprei, Sebstain, *The Tribes of North East India*, Vendrame Missiological Insitute, Shillong, 1984.

Karve, D.G. *Poverty and Population in India*, Oxford Univ. Press London, 1936.

Kaith, D.C., *Shifting Cultivation Practices in India* (A review), U.N. Chatterjee Indian Council of Agricultural Research, New Delhi, 1958.

Kapadia, K.M., *The Matrilineal Social Organisation of the Nagas of Assam*, Bombay, 1950.

Kapoor D. & Chopra, S.R.K., *Ethnic and Cultural Units of Lahaul*, (Presented in the seminar on Tribal Situation in India, Indian Institute of Advance Study, Simla), 1969.

Kattakayam, Jacob, *Social Structure & Chance Among the Trible*, D.K. Publishers Distributors (P) Ltd., New Delhi, 1982.

Kaul, S.K., *Tribal Art & Handicrafts*, Bharatiya Adimjati Sevak Sangh, New Delhi, 1954.

Kayastha, S.L., *The Himalayan Beas Basin: Study in Habitat, Economy and Society*, Banaras Hindu University, Bananasi, 1964.

Kayastha, S.L., *Geography and Environment: Issues and Challenges*, Naurang Rai, Concept Publishing company H-13, Bali Nagar, New Delhi-110015, India.

Kellogg, C.E., *Soil and Land Classification*, Tour of Farm Eco., 1951.

Khan, Ahmed, *The Chenchus*, Indian Science Congress, 1982.

Kitts, J., *A Compendium of the Castes and Tribes found in India*, D.K. Publishers, New Delhi.

Kothari, K.L., *Tribal Social Change in India*, D.K. Publishers, New Delhi.

Krishnan, Nanboodri, *Social System and Human Fertility toward a Theoritical Framework*, University of Michingan, 1963.

Kshetri, Rajendra, *Polity Formation Among the Tribes of Manipur: A Preliminary Survey of the Moyon and Paite Polity*, Centre for Tribal Studies, M.U. 1990. Imphal.

Kulachandra Pandit, *Meitei Lai Haraoba*, D. Gandhi Memorial Press, Imphal, 1963.

Kulirani, B. Francis, *Impact of Cash Crop Economy on the Tribes of Wyand.*

Kulkarni, M.G., *Problems of Tribal India*, D.K. Publishers, New Delhi.

Kloss, B.C., *In the Andamans and Nicobars*, London, 1903.

Kumar, Pramod, *Folk Icons and Rituals in Tribal Life*, Abhinav Publication, New Delhi-16, 1984.

Kuton, C.L., *King Thebaw and the Ecological Rape of Burma*, New Delhi, 1974.

Kumar, Alok, *Tribal Culture and Economy: The Mal Paharias of Santal Parganas*, D.K. Publishers, New Delhi.

Kuty, A.R., *Marriage and Kinship in an Island Society*, National Publishing House, New Delhi.

Kuznets, Siman, *Economic Growth and Structure*, Oxford and IBH Publishing Co., New Delhi, 1974.

Lorrain J.H. & Savidge F.W., *The Lushai Grammar and Dictionary*, D.K. Publishers Distributors (P) Ltd., New Delhi.

Lakdawala, D.T., Alag, Y.K. & Sharma, Atul, *Regional Variation in Industrial Development*, Sardar Patel Institute of Economic and Social Research, Ahmedabad, 1974.

Lal, R.B., *A Comparative Study of Traditional Panch and Statutory Panchayat*, Tribal Reseach and Training Institute, Gujarat Budyapith, Ahmedabad.

Lal, S. K. & Nahar Umed Raj, *Higher Education Scheduled Castes & Scheduled Tribes*, D. K. Publishers. New Delhi .

Lall, P., *Kumaon Local Customs*, Govt. Press, Allahabad, 1921.

Latham, R. G., *Ethnology of India*, Vass Voorst, London, 1859.

Latham, R. G., *Tribes and Races Vol* –II 1983 (1850) Cultural Publishing House, New Delhi.

Lehar, Ethnic Group of Mainland South East Asia.

Lehman, F. K., *The Structure of Chin Society*, The Univ. of Illinois Press, Urband, 1963.

Leith-Rose, Sylvia, *African Woman*, Routledge & Kegan Paul, London, 1939.

Leland Donald (ed.) *These in Ethnology* and Culture History Archana Publications, Meerut, 1987.

Lerner, D., *The Passing Away of the Traditional Society*, New York, 1964.

Leuva, K. K., *The Asur: A Study of Primitive Iron Smithers*, Bharatiya Adimjati Sevak Sangh, N. Delhi, 1963.

Levi-Strauss, *C. The Savage Mind*, 1966, London.

Lewin, Thomas, *Wild Hill Tracts of Chittagong & the Dwellers Therein*, Calcutta, 1869.

Leim, Z. Z., *The U-Now People*, 1981, Churachandpur, Manipur .

Leire, W. J., *Survey of Soil; Present land use and land Capabilities of the Terich FAO- ETAP* Report No. 1965.

Light Foot, Louise, *Dance Rituals of Manipur*, India, The Standard Press, Hong Kong, 1958.

Lingaiah, Karanti, *Industrialisation in Tribal Areas*, D. K. Publishers, Delhi.

Lish, A. B., *A Brief Acount of the Khasees*, Calcutta Christian Observer, Vol. VII, Calcutta, 1838.

Lubbok, J., *The Origin of Civilization and Primitive condition of Man*, London, 1870.

Luikham, R., *Folklore and Tales of the Nagas*, Emmanuel Publishers-Printers, New Delhi, 1987.

Luikham, S., *A Short History of the Manipur Baptist Christain Jubilee*, Ukhrul, 1948.

Luikham, T., *Wung* (Tangkhul) *Naga*, Imphal, Tarun Printing Works, 1961.

L. Luingam & Nandita Haksar, *Nagaland File: A Question of Human Rights* New Delhi,1984.

Luiz A.A.D., *Tribes of Kerala*, Bharatiya Adimjati Sewak Sangh, New Delhi, 1962.

Lukacs, John R (ed) *The people of South Asia*, 1984. Plenum Press, New York.

Maasorang A. O., *Social and Cultural Changes in the Tribal Communities Today and Responsibility of the Churches*, Religion and Society, Vol. IX.

Meekenfie. A., *The North East Frontier of India*, Delhi Mittal Publication, 1981 (Rep.).

Mahapatra, Sitakant, *Modernization and Ritual, Identity and Change in Santal Society*, D. K. Publishers Distributors, (P) Ltd. Delhi.

MaCall, Major Anthony Gilchrist, *Lushai Chrysalis*, Luzac & Co. Ltd. London, 1949.

McCulloch, Major W., *Account of the Valley of Manipur and of the Hill Tribes*, Calcutta, Bengal Printing Co. 1859, Delhi, Gian Publications, 1980 (Rep.).

McGourdon, Janet, B. Montgovery, *Among the Head Hunters of Formosa*, Small, Magnard & Boston, 1922.

Mahanta, J., *Mental Health and Achievement Motivation of the Juang tribe in a Changing Socio Cultural Setting.* Doctoral Thesis Submitted to Utkal Univ. (Unpublished), 1971.

Mahapatra, E.K., *A Hill Bhuiya Village:An Empirical Socio-Economic Study*, Phil. Dissertotoon, Homburg, 1959.

Maine, H.J.S., *Dissertions of Early Law and Custom*, New York, 1886.

Majid Husain, *Agricultural Geography*, Inter-India Publication, New Delhi, 1979.

Majumdar, D.N. and Datta Roy, B., *Tribal Occupational Mobility*, Research India Publications, Calcutta, 1984.

Majumdar, D. N. et. al., *Social Custom of an Industrial City, Social Survey of Kanpur*, 1954-56, Asia publishing House, Bombay, 1960.

Majumdar, D.N., *Himalayan Polyandry*, Asia Publishing House, Bombay, 1963.

Majumdar, D.N., *Fortunes of the Primitive Tribes*, The Universal Publishers Ltd. Lucknow, 1944.

Majumdar, D. N., *A Tribe in Transition: A Study in Culture Pattern*, Longmans Green & Co. London, 1937.

Majumdar, D.N., *The Affairs of a Tribe: A Study in Tribal Dynamics*, Universal Publishers Ltd. Lucknow, 1950b.

Majumdar, D.N., *The Garos (an account of the Garos of the Present day)*, The Lawyers Book Stall, Gauhati, 1956.

Malinowski, B., *Sex and Repression in Savages Society*, London, 1927.

Malinowski, B., *Dynamics of Culture Change*, London, 1961.

Malsawna, J. *Zo Nun* (The Life Style of the Mizo People) The Ziki Printing Press, Aijawl, 1963.

Man, E. H., *On The Aboriginal Inhabitants of the Andaman Islands*, London, m. d. (1885).

Man, E.G., *Sonthalia and the Sonthals*, Mital Publications, New Delhi- 25, 1983.

Mandal, R.B., *Land Utilization: Theory and Practice*, Naurang Rai, Concept Publishing Co. H-13. Bali Nagar, New Delhi-15

Mandal, R.B., *Tribals at the Polls; A Study of Khunti in Chotanagpur*, D.K. Publishers, New Delhi.

Mankekar, D. R., *On the Slippery Slope in Nagaland*, P.C. Manaktala and Sons Private Ltd., 6 Fiar Field, Road No.4, Chunchgate, Bombay-1, 1967.

Mann, K., *Trible Woman in a Changing Society*, Tribes of India Series, D. K. Publishers, New Delhi.

Mann, R. S. (ed.) *Nature- Man-Spirit Complex in Tribal India*, Concept Publishing Company, New Delhi, 1981.

Marshal, W.E., *Travel Among the Todas for the Study of Primitive Tribes in South India: Their History, Characters, Custom, Religion, Infanticides, Polyandry, Language, With Outlines of the Toda Grammer*, Longmans Green and Co. London, 1873.

Mathew, J. (ed.) *Tribal Economy of North East Region, Gauhati*, Spectrum Publication, 1980.

Mathur, P.R.G. *The Khasi of Meghalaya*, Cosmo Publication, New Delhi, 1979.

Mathur, L.P., *Resistance Movement of Tribals of India A Case Study of Bhils of Rajasthan in the 19th Century*, D.K. Publishers, Delhi.

Mawrie,H.O., *The Khasi Miliew*, Concept Publishing Company, New Delhi-15, 1981.

Meerwarth, A.M., *The Andamanes, Nicobarase and Hill Tribes of Assam*, Spectrum Publications, Pan Bazar, Gauhati, 1980 (1919).

Mehta, B.H., *Social and Economic Conditions of Chodras*, An Aboriginal Tribe of Gujarat, 1933, (M.A.1933).

Mehta, B.H., *Gonds and the Gondwana Land* (The Report Submitted to the planning Commission, Unpub.)1968.

Meitei Bharat P., *Kakching Haraoba*, Manipur, M.G. Singh Printer, Kakching Bazar, 1977.

Mitchell, Capt St. John F., *The North-East Frontier of India*, Vivek Publishing House,18D, Kamla Nagar, Delhi, Ist Pub. 1883, Reprint of 1973.

Mills, J.P., *The Lhota Nagas*, London, MacMillan & Co. ltd. 1922.

Mills, J.P., *The Rengma Nagas*, Spectrum Publications, Pan Bazar Gauhati-1, 1980 (1937.)

Mills, J.P., Folk Stories of Lhota Naga, 1987.

Mills, J.P., *The Ao Nagas*, Oxford Univ. Press, London W-1, Oxford House, Applo Bunder, Bonleoy 400001. 1973 (2nd Edition).

Millington, P., *On the Truck of the Abor*, London, 1912.

Mishra, P.K. and Others (ed.) *Tribes of Southern Region: A Select biblicgraphy*, D.K. Publishers (P) Ltd. Delhi.

Mishra, K.C. *Tribes in the Mahabharata, A Socio-Cultural Study*, Delhi, National Printing House, 1987.

Mishra, S.N. and Bhupinder Singh, (ed.), *Tribal Area Development*, SSRD, New Delhi-14, 1983

Mishra, S.N. and Prasad, L.M., *Tribal Voting Behaviour: A Study of Bihar Tribes*, D.K. Publishers, New Delhi.

Mishra, U., *North-East India: Quest for Identity*, 1988.

Mitchell, J.C. *Tribalism and Plural Society*, Oxford Univ. Press, London, 1960.

Mitra, Ashok, *India and Population, Aspects of Quality and Control*, Vols. I & II, Abhiman Publication, New Delhi, 1978.

Mitra, Ashok, *Special Tables for Scheduled Castes & Schedued Tribes, Census of India, 1961*, Vol. I, Pf. U-A, Manager of Publication, Delhi

Mitra, Rathin & Barun Das Gupta, (eds), *A Common Perspective for North East India*, Navana Printing Works, Ltd. Calcutta, 1967.

Mohan, N. Shantha, *Status of Banjara Women in India*, D.K. Publishers Distributors (P) Ltd., New Delhi..

Mohanta, Bijan, *Administrative Development of Arunachal Pradesh 1975*. Uppal Publishing House, 3 Ansari Road, Daryaganj, New Delhi-110002.

Mohapatra, P.C., *Economic Development of Tribal India*, D.K. Publishers Distributors (P) Ltd., New Delhi..

Morris, C.J., *Living with the Lepchas : A Book About Sikkim*, Himalayas, Toronoto Heinemann, London, 1938.

Mukerjee, R.K., *Food Planning for four Hundred Millions*, MacMillan & Co. London 1938.

Mukerjee, C. L., *The Santhal*, A.R. Mukherjee, Calcutta, 1939.

Mukhopadhyay, SanKarananda, *The Austrices of India*, 1975, K.P. Bagchi & Co Calcutta-12.

Myrdal Gunnar, *Asian Drama*, An Enquiry into the poverty of Nations, Vols. I, II, & III. Kalyani Publishers, New Delhi, Ludhiana.

Niswas, Dipti Kumar., *Society Polity and Economy, An Inter-Disciplinary Approach*, D.K. Publishers Distributors (P) Ltd., New Delhi..

Nader, A., *Bio-Economic Problem of India-India's Population Problem from a New Angle of View*, Vidya Mandir, New Delhi, 1940.

Nag, D.S., Tribal Economy: *An Economic Study of the Baiga*, Bhartiya Adimjati Sevak Sangh, Delhi, 1958.

Nair, M.K. Sukumaran, *Tribal Economy in Transition : A Study of Meghalaya*, D.K. Publishers Distributors (P) Ltd., New Delhi.-7.

Nakene, Chie, *Economic and Social Structure of Lepcha Bhutia of Central Sikkim, Rural Society in Sikkim -- A Study of the Inter-relations of Lepcha, Bhotias. and Nepalis in Caste and Kin In Nepal*, India and Ceylon, Edited by C. Van-Furer Haimendorf, Asia Publishing House. Bombay, 1966, 2-13-263.

Nakene, Chie, Garo and Khasi: *A comparative Study in Matrilineal Systems*, Paris, The Haque: Mouton & Co., 1967.

Naik, T.B., *Impact of Education on the Bhils*, planning Commission, New Delhi, 1969a.

Naik, T.B., *Raja Hirdeshah:A tribal Play*, Tribal Research Institute, Chhindwara, Unpublished, 1963.

Naik, T.B., *The Abhujh Marias*, Tribal Research Institute, Chhindwara, 1963.

Naik, T.B., *The Bhil: A Study*, Bhartiya Adimjati Sevak Sangh, New Delhi, 1956.

Naik, T.B. and Bhauraskar, K.K., *Changing Tribes*, Tribal Research Institute, Chhindwara, 1961.

Narain, Vatsala & Prakasan, C.P., *Population Policy Perspectives in Developing Countries*, Himalayan Publishing House, Bomday, 1983.

Narayan, Sachindra, *A Dwindling Hill Tribe of Bihar* D.K. Publishers Distributors (P) Ltd., New Delhi-7.

Narayan, Sachindra, *Dimensions of Development in Tribal Bihar*, D.K. Publishers Distributors (P) Ltd., New Delhi-7.

Narayan, Sachindra, *Movements Development : Policy and Judiciary in Tribal World*, Inter-India Publications, New Delhi.

Narayan, S., *Tribe in Transition*, Inter-India Publications, New Delhi.

Nari, R., *Enchanted Frontier*, Oxford University Press, 1971.

Natarjan, Nalini, *The Missionary Among the Khasis*, Sterling Publishing Pvt. Ltd. New Delhi-16, 1977.

National Council of Applied Ecocomic Research, *Techno-Economic Survey of Manipur*, Manipur Administration, Imphal, 1961.

Nath, Y.V.S., Bhils of Ratanmal – *An Analysis of the Social Structure of A Western Indian Community*, Baroda, The Maharaja Sayajirao University, 1960.

Negi, B.S., *Rural Geography*, Kedar Nath Ram Nath College Road, Meerut-250001, U.P.

Negi, B.S., *Soil Types, Fertility and Land Use in Garhwal District*, Geog. Rev. Indian 1978.

Negi, S.S., *Tribal Welfare Development and Administration*, D.K. Publishers Distributors (P) Ltd., New Delhi.

Negi, Thakur Sen, *Scheduled Tribes of Himachal Pradesh*, ThakurSen Negi, Simla, 1976.

Neiggemeir, H., *Kuttia Khond of Orissa*, Frobenius Institute, Frankfurt, 1964.

Nibedon, Nirmal, *Mizoram, The Dagger Bridge*, Lancers Publishers, P.O. Box No. 4235, New Delhi-110028, 2nd Edition, 1983, (1st Edition 1980).

Nibedon, Nirmal, *North East India, The Ethnic Explosion*, Lancers Publishers, P.O. Box No. 4235, New Delhi-110048, India.

Nibedon, Nirmal, *Nagaland: The Night of the Guerrilas.*

North Eastern Council, *Shifting Cultivation in the North Eastern India*, Shillong, 1983.

Oakley, E.S., *Holy Himalayas*, Anderson and Ferrier, London, 1905.

Orans, Martin, The Santal: *A Tribe in Search of a Great Tradition*, Detroit, Wayne University Press, 1965.

Owen, J., *Notes on the Naga Tribes in Communication with Assam*, Calcutta, 1844.

Pachauri, S.K., *Dynamics of rural Development in Tribal Areas – A Study of Srikakulam District, Andhra Pradesh*, Concept Publishing Company, New Delhi, 1984.

Padgi, S.R., Among the Gonds of Adilabad, Bombay, 11 ed., 1952.

Padhy, K.S. and P.S. *Tribal India*, A Newsletter No. 75, Central News Agency (P) Ltd., 23/90, Connaught Circus, New Delhi, 1989.

Panchani, *Manipur: Religion, Culture and Society.*

Pant, S.D., '*Socio-Economic Life of the Kumaon Village* (Master's thesis submitted at Lucknow University, Delhi-52, 1928, 1935.

Pareek, R.N. *Tribal Culture in flux*, B.R. Publishing Corporation, Delhi-52, 1977.

Paravathamma, C. *Scheduled Castes and Tribes*, D.K. Publishers Distributors (P) Ltd., New Delhi..

Parratt, Saroj Nalini, *The Religion of Manipur*, Firma K.L.M. Private Ltd. Calcutta, 1980.

Parry, N.E., *The Lakhers*, Macmillan & Co., London, 1932.

Parry, N.E., *Lushai Custom: A Monograph on Lushai* Trina KLN Private Ltd. 1976.

Patel, G.D., *Land System of the Union Territories of India*, Charotar Book Stall Tulsi Sadan st. (W.RLY) India, 1970.

Patel, M.L., *Agro-Economic Problems of India*

Patel, M.L., *Agro-Economic Survey of Tribal Mandla*, Prople's Publishing House, New Delhi, 1969.

Patel, M.L., *Factors Influenceing change of the Pattern of Tribal Areas of Madhya Pradesh*, 1980.

Patel, M.L., *Focus on protection of Land Ownership Rights of Tribal*, Vanyerjatie New Delhi, 1973.

Patel, M.L., *Land Problems of Scheduled Tribes in India*, Girivanvasi Sandesh, Bombay, 1974

Patel, M.L., *Planning Strategy for Tribal Development*, Inter-India Publications, New Delhi-15. 1984.

Patel, M.L., *Protection of Tribal Rights in Lands*, Girivanvasi Sandesh, Bombay.

Patel, Srisha, *Ecology, Ethnology & Nutrition: A Study of Kondh Tribals & Tebetan Refugees.*, D.K. Publishers Distributors (P) Ltd., New Delhi.

Patel, Tara, *Development of Education Among Tribal Women*, D.K. Publishers Distributors (P) Ltd., New Delhi..

Pathy, Jaganath, *Under Development and Destitution:Essays on Orissan Society*, Tribal Studies of India Series, T 132. D.K. Publishers Distributors (P) Ltd., New Delhi..

Pathak, K.B., *On the Mechanism of Selection of Fecundability*, IIPS, Bombay, 1970.

Pathy, Jaganath, *Tribal Peasantry Dynamic of Development*, Inter-India Publication, New Delhi, 1984.

Pati, R.N. & Jena B., *Tribal Development in India*, Tripathi Book Service, Karol Bagh, New Delhi, 1989.

Patnaik, U.N., *A Saora House*, 1964-65, 49-50.

Paul M.C., *Dimensions of Tribal Movements in India: A Study of Udayachal in Assam Valley*, 1989.

Payeng, H., *Economic and Social Change in India*, 1988.

Pemberton, R.B., *The Eastern Frontier of India*, Delhi, Mittal Pub. 1979 (Rep.)

Perry, W.J. *The Childern of the Sun*, London, 1923.

Peterson, W., *Population*, The Macmillan Co. London, 1969.

Pettigrew, W., *Tangkhul Naga Grammar*, Shillong, 1918.

Pingle, U., B.N. Mukherjee and S.K. Das, *A Genetical Study of the five Tribal Group of Andhra Pradesh, India*, 1981.

Phipson, S.S. *Tribal Beliefs on Tuberculosis in the Hills and Frontier Tracts of Assam*, Shillong, 1939.

Playfair, A., *The Garos*, United Publishers Gauhati-1, 1975.

Pledger, W.F., The Bhils, A Brief Anthropological Study, Ph. D. Dissertation Submitted to Harford Seminary Foundation, Kenedy School of Mission, 1944.

Portman, M.V., *History of Our Relations with the Andamanese*, 2 Vols. Compiled from Historical and Travels and from Records of the Govt. of India, Superintendent Printing Press, Calcutta, 1889.

Portman, M.V., *A Manual of the Andaman Language*, London, 1887.

Portman, M.V. *The Andaman Islanders*, 15 Yels. Calcutta, 1871-94, (Privately Printed)

Pothan, S.G., *The Syrian Christians of Kerala*, 1963, Asia Publishing House, New Delhi.

Prabhakara, N.R., *Internal Migration and Population Redistribution in India*, (Some Reflections), Concept Publishing Co., New Delhi, 1986.

Praharaj, Denendra Mohan, *Tribal Movement and Political History in India: A Case Study from Orissa, 1803-1949*. Tribal Studies in India Series: T-127. D.K. Publishers Distributors (P) Ltd., New Delhi..

Prasad, Maheswari, *Tribes: Their Environment and Culture*, D.K. Publishers, Delhi.

Prasad, Maheswari, *Social Aspects of Mining Towns of the Tribal Religion* (in 2 Parts). D.K. Publishers Distributors (P) Ltd., New Delhi.

Prasad, Maheswari, *Tribal Geography, 1979*, Classical Publication, New Delhi.

Parasad, N., *Land and People of Tribal Bihar*, Tribal Welfare Research Institute, Ranchi, 1964.

Prasad, Onkar, *Santal Music: A Study in Pattern and Process of Cultural Perlistance*, D.K. Publishers Distributors (P) Ltd., New Delhi..

Prasad, R.K., *Economic and social Change among the Parahiyas of Palaman - A Study in Tribal Dynamics* (Ph. D. Thesis, Ranchi University, Unpublished).

Prasad S.D., *Village Survey Monograph on Kumar Bhaja, Both Banga and Jamkanali*, 1961, Superintendent of Census, Bihar, 4(1-4), Bihar Part-VI).

Pratap, D.R., *Plan for Development of the Chenches*, Hyderbad, 1976.

Pressat, Roland, *Statistical Demography*, Methuen & Co. Ltd. 1978.

Prongo, K. (ed) *The Nagas*, Imphal, 1981.

Pudaite, R., *The Education of the Hmar People*, Sielment, Imphal, 1963.

Pugh, B.M., *The Story of Tribal, 1976*, Orient Longman Limited, Calcutta.

Rabha, Rajen, *Tabha Janajali*, Jorhat Assam Society Sabha, Assam, 1974.

Radcliffe-Brown,A.R., *The Andman Islanders*, Cambridge, 1933.

The Social organization of Austrilian Tribes, *Oceania Monograph*, No. I, Sydeny, 1931.

Rai, B.K., Nature and Man: A Study of Interaction Between Man and Forest in Chotanagpur, Doctoral Dissertation, Ranchi University Unpublished, 1967.

Raizada, Ajit, *Tribal Development in Madhya Pradesh*, Inter-India Publications, New Delhi, 1984.

Raja Moonis and Aijaz Ahamed, *General Geography of India*, National Council of Educational Research and Training, 1978.

Rajagopal, *Dynamics of Agricultural Marketing in Tribal India*, D.K. Publisher Distributors (P) Ltd. Delhi.

Ramunny, M., *The World of Nagas*, 1988.

Ramaiah, P., *Tribal Economy of India: A Case of Koyas of Andhra Pradesh*, D.K. Publishers Distributors (P) Ltd., New Delhi..

Ramaiah, P., *Issues in Tribal Development*, D.K. Publishers Distributors (P) Ltd., New Delhi..

Ramakant, *Tribes: A Study in Cultural Ecology and Tribal Dynamics of the Parahiya*, D.K. Publishers Distributors (P) Ltd., New Delhi..

Ramamani, V.S., *Tribal Economy Problems and Prospects*, D.K. Publishers Distributors (P) Ltd., New Delhi..

Rao, Adityendra, *Tribal Social Stratification*, D.K. Publishers Distributors (P) Ltd., New Delhi..

Rao, I. Murali, Krishna, *Marketing in Tribal Economy: A Study with Special Reference to Shandies (Periodic Market) in the Movements*, (2Vols.). D.K. Publishers Distributors (P) Ltd., New Delhi..

Rao, M.S.A. (ed), *Social Movements in India: Peasant and Backward Classes*, 2nd Edition Movements, Sectorian, Tribal and Women's Movements (2 Vols.) D.K. Publishers Distributors (P) Ltd., New Delhi..

Rao, P.V., *Institutional Frame Works for Tribal Development*, D.K. Publishers Distributors (P) Ltd., New Delhi..

Rao, K. Prakash, *Ethnographic Study with Special Reference to Social Organisation, Myths and Ritual and Cultural Change*, 1952-53.

Rasvi, Mujtaba, *The Frontiers of Pakistan*, National Publishing House Ltd. Karachi-Dacca, 71.

Rathmiah, E.V., *Structure Constrains in Tribal Education: A Regional Study*, Sterling Publishers, Pvt. Ltd. New Delhi, 1977.

Ray, P.C., *The Lodha and their Spirit Possessed Men: A Psycho-Socio-Cultural Study*, Anthropological Survey of India, Calcutta, 1965.

Rayappa, P.H., *Backwardness and Welfare of Scheduled Caste and Scheduled Tribes in India*, D.K. Publishers Distributors (P) Ltd., New Delhi..

Reddy, G.P., *The Chenchus, A Scheduled Tribe of Andhra Pradesh*, Delhi, 1964.

Reddy, P.C., The Yanadis of Madras Presidency (Ph.D. Thesis, Lucknow University, Unpublished) 1940a.

Reddy, G.P., *Politics of Tribal Exploitation : A Study unrest in Adilabad*. D.K. Publishers Distributors (P) Ltd., New Delhi..

Reddy, G.P. (ed.), *Studies in Island Cultures of India*, D.K. Publishers Distributors (p) Ltd. Delhi.

Reid, Robert, *History of the Frontier Areas Boardering on Assam 1883-1941*, Eastern Publishing House, 6-A Banarsi Das Market, Tinapur, Delhi-7, Reprinted, 1983.

Rele, J.R. & Jain S.K. (ed.), *Population Change and Rural Development in India*, IIPS, Bombay, 1918.

Reid Robert, *Years of Change in Bengal and Assam*, London, 1966.

Rink, H.J., *The Eskimo Tribes*, 1887, London.

Risely, H.H., *The Tribes and Castes of Bengal*, 4 Vols. Calcutta, 1891.

Rivenburg, N. (ed.) *The Star of the Naga Hills: Letters from Rev. Sidney and H. Rivenburg*, Pioneer Missionaries in Assam, 1883-1923, Philadelphia, 1941.

Rivers, W.H.R, *The Todas*, Macmillan and Co., Ltd. London, 1906.

Rizvi, S.H.M., *Mina: The Rulling Tribe of Rajasthan Socio-Biological Appraisal*, 1987.

Robinson, W., *A Descriptive Account of Assam to which is added a short Account of the Neighbour Tribes*, Ostell and Lapage, London, 1841.

Roel, Wirngam Egbert, Kartu Nitor Chara & Ngamshing Ngaru, (eds.), *A History of the Mon Naga Church 1925-75* (in Meitei language), Komlathabi Baptist Church, Manipur, 1975.

Romaiah, P., *Tribal Economy of India: A Case Study of Koyos of Andhra Pradesh*, Light and Light Publications, New Delhi, 1981.

Rose, H.A., *A Glossary of the Tribes and Castes of Punjab and North Eastern Frontier Province*, 1914, 14.

Rose, Leo E and Fisher, Magaret W., *The North East Frontier Agency of India*, California, 1967.

Roy Burman B.K., *Demographic and Socio-Economic: Profiles of the Hill areas of North East India*, Office of the Registrar General India, New Delhi, 1970.

Roy Burman B.K., *Encouragement to Tribal Arts and Handicrafts, Report of the Third Conference for Tribes and Tribal (Scheduled) Areas*, Jabalpur, 1955.

Roy Burman B.K., *Social Demography in India*, Review Report submitted to the Indian Council for Social Science Research, New Delhi, 1969.

Roy, HL Deb, *A Tribe in Transition*, Cosmo Publications, New Delhi, 1981.

Roy, HL Deb, *Tribe in Transition: The Jaintias of Meghalaya.*

Roy, J., *History of Manipur*, Calcutta, East Light Book Frontier Agency, Shillong, 196[illegible].

Roy, Sachin, *Aspects of Padam Minyong Culture*, North East Frontier Agency, Shillong, 1960.

Roy, Sarat Chandra, *The Mundas and Their Country*, Asia Publishing House, Bombay, 1970.

Roy, Sarat Chandra, *The Granons of Chotangpur*, Ranchi Bar Library, Ranchi, 1915 a.

Roy, S.C., *The Birhor: A Little Known Jungle Tribe of Chotanaqpur*, Man in India Office, Ranchi, 1925a.

Roy, S.C., *The Hill Bhuiyas of Orissa, Man in India Office*, Ranchi, 1935.

Roy, S.C. and Hira Lal, R.B., *The Khatia*, Man in India Office, Ranchi, 1937.

Russel, R.V. & Hira Lal, R.B., *Tribes & Castes of the Central Provinces of India*, 4 Vols. London, 1906.

Rymhai, H., *The Birth of Seinraj: Khasi Heritage*, Shillong, 1969.

Rymhai, T., *Certain Customs of the Pnars and their Changing patterns: Khasi Heritage*, Shillong 1969.

Rymhai, T. *et al.*, *Report on the Land Reforms Commission for Khasi Hills*, Shillong, 1974.

Sachchidananda *et al.* (ed)., *Tradition and Development*, D.K. Publishers Distributors (P) Ltd. Delhi.

Sachchidananda, *Culture Change in Tribal Bihar*, Bookland Private Ltd. Calcutta, 1964.

Sachchidananda, *The Tribal Village in Bihar: A Study in Unity and Extension*, Oriental Publishers, New Delhi, 1968.

Sachchidananda and Mandal B.B., *Industrialisation and Social Disorganisation : A Study of Tribals in Bihar*, D.K. Publishers Distributors (P) Ltd., New Delhi..

Sahay, B.N., *Dynamics of Leadership*, Book Hive, New Delhi, 1968.

Sahay, K.N., *Change of Tribal Identity in Chotanagpur*, Varanasi, Kishore Vidya Niketon, Varanasi, 1985.

Saigal, Omesh, *Tripura: Its History and Culture*, Concept Publishing Com. Delhi, 1978.

Saksena, R.N., *Social Economy of a Polyandrous People*, Asia Publishing company, (Delhi) Bombay, 1962.

Saksena, R.P. *Tribal Economy in Central India*, Firma K.L. Mukhopadhyaya, Cal. 1964.

Saksena, H.S. *Safeguards for Scheduled Castes and Scheduled Tribes: Founding Father Views*, D.K. Publishers Distributors (P) Ltd., New Delhi.

Samuelson, Ramchuani Sena, *Love Mizoram*, Goodwill Press Imphal, 1985.

Sangma, M.S., *History and Culture of the Garos*, D.K. Publishers Distributors (P) Ltd., New Delhi..

Sardeshpande, S.C., *The Patkoi Nagas*, 1987.

Sarkar J., *Tribal Mobility in Tribal*, Madhya Publishing Corporation, Delhi.

Sarkar, S.S., *The Maler of Rajmahal Hills*, Book Co. Calcutta, 1938.

Sarin, V.I.K., *India's North-East in Flames*, Shibadab, Ghaziabad, Tarang Paperbacks, 1982.

Sarin, K.A., *Nilakanta* MANARTALAS Bombay, 1967.

Sauar, C.O., *Mapping the Utilization of Land*, 1919.

Save, K.J., *The Worlis*, Bombay, 1945.

Saveaora, K.J., *The Worli: A Study of and Aboriginal Tribe of Bombay Presidency*, Padma Publishing Co. Bombay, 1945.

Saxena, Ranbir Prakash, *Tribal Economy in Central India*, Firma K.L. Mukhopadhyaya, Calcutta, 1964.

Schapera, I., *Government and Politics in Tribal Society*, London, 1956.

Schilipp, P.D., *Shifting Cultivation in Africa (The Azdnde System of Agriculture)*, Routledge and Kegan Paul, London, 1956.

Sen, G.N., *The Primary Education for Tribals*, Report of the Second conference for Tribes and Tribal (Schi) Areas, Bharatiya Adimjati Sevak Sangha, Delhi, 1953, 135-136.

Sen, S., *Arunachal Pradesh and the Tribes : Select Bibliography.*

Sen, Souman, *Folk-Lore in North-East India*, Omsons Publication, Gauhati, 1985.

Sen, S., *Between Tradition and Change : A perspective of Meghalaya*, 1988.

Sen, Sipra, *Tribes of Nagaland*, D.K. Publishers Distributors (P) Ltd., New Delhi., 1987.

Sen, Sipra, *Tribes of Meghalaya*, D.K. Publishers Distributors (P) Ltd., New Delhi..

Sen, S., *Social and State Formation in Khasi Jaintia Hills : A Study of folk-Lore*, 1985.

Shadap-Sen, Namita Catherine, *The Origin and Early Histroy of the Khasi-Synteng Peoples*, Firma KLM Private Ltd., Calcutta, 1981.

Shafi, M., Techniques of Rural Land Use Planning with reference to India, *Geographer* 13, 1966.

Shafi, M., *Land Use Studies : A Trend Report, A Survey of Research in Geography*, Popular Prakashan, Bombay,1972.

Shah, Ghanasyam, *Politics of Scheduled Castes and Tribes*, Vora & Co. Publishers Pvt. Ltd. Bombay, 1975.

Shah, Ghanashyam, *Economic Differentiations and Tribal Identity*, 1984, Ajanta Publication, Delhi.

Shah, G. *et al.*, *Tribal Education in Gujarat*, D.K. Publishers Distributors (P) Ltd., New Delhi..

Shah, P.C., Dabla, *Gujarat Research Society*, Bombay, 1958.

Shah, P.C., *Tribal Life in Gujarat*, Gujarat Research Society, Bombay, 1959

Shah, P.C., *Naikas-Naikdas : A Gujarat Tribe*, Gujarat Research Society, Bombay, 1959.

Shah, V.P. and Patel, Tara, *Social Contexts of Tribal Education*, D.K. Publishers Distributors (P) Ltd. Delhi.

Shakespear, J., *The Lushai Kuki Clans*, Cultural Publishing House, Delhi, 1912.

Shakespear, L.W., *History of Assam Rifles*, Mrs. Suman Lata, Caltural Publishing House, 18d, Kamla Nagar, Delhi-7, 1929, First Pub. 1983. (Rep.)

Shakespear, L.W., *History of Upper Assam, Upper Burma & North Eastern Frontier*, London, 1914.

Sharan, Mahesh Kumar, *Tribal Coins - A Study*, Abhinav Publications, New Delhi, 1972.

Sharma, A.C., *Analysis of the Population Growth in Assam 1951-61*, IIPS Bombay, 1964.

Sharma, B.B.L., *Simple Economics of Population Control*, Central Family Planning Institute, New Delhi,1970.

Sharma, RR. P. *The People of NEFA: The Sherdukepens*, Shillong, NEFA Administration, 1961.

Sharma, B.D., *Occasional Paper on Tribal Development*, Series 1-12, Govt. Of India, New Delhi, 1876.

Sharma, B.D., *Planning for Tribal Development*, Prachi Prakashan, New Delhi, 1984.

Sharma, B.D., *Tribal Development*, Prachi Prakashan, New Delhi, 1978.

Sharma, B.D., *Tribal Woman in the Whirl of Change: A Saga Administration Transition*, New Delhi, 1988.

Sharma, Nandalal, *Meitrabak*, Imphal, 1960.

Sharma, F. Iboton. *Meitel Fijet Leiteng*, Imphal.

Sharma R.N. and Santosh *Tribes and Tribal Development*, Uppal Publishang House, Bakshi, New Delhi, 1984.

Sharma, D.K., *Education and Socialization Among the Tribes*, D.K. Publishers Distributors (P) Ltd. New Delhi

Shashi, S.S., *The Nomads of the Himalayas*, Sundeep Prakashan, Delhi, 1979.

Shasmal, K.C., Bauris of West Bengal (Ph.D. Thesis Calcutta University, Calcutta, Unpub.) 1967.

Shastri, a. Banerji, *The Nagas, Annalas of Bhandarker Oriental Research Institute*, Vol. XVIII, 1938.

Shaw. L.M., *Shifting Cultivation: Tropical Agriculture*, 1957.

Shaw, William, *The Thadou Kukis*, Caltural Publishing House, Delhi, 1983 (1929).

Sherring, Rev. M A., *Hindu Tribes and Castes*, Vol. I, II, III, Cosmo Publishang, 10178,Library Road, Delhi-110006, 1st Pub. London, 1872.

Shimmi, L. Ronald, *Comparative History of the Nagas from Ancient Period Till 1826*, D. K Publishers Distributors (p) Ltd. Delhi.

Shimmi, YLR., *Comparative History of Nagas: From Ancient Period Till 1826*, 1988.

Shimmi, M.K., *Tangkhul Miwurlung*, Imphal, Bhagyabati Karayalaya Churachang Printing Works, 1967.

Shimray, R.R., *Origin and Calture of Nagas*, published by Mrs. Pamleiphi Shimary, C-4 Moti bagh II, New Delhi-110021.

Shukla, H.L. *Tribal Heritage of madhay Pradesh : An Annotated Bibliography*, D.K. Publishers Destributors (P) Ltd. Delhi.

Shukla, H.L., *Tribal History: A New Interpretation*, D.K. Publishers Distoibutors (P) Ltd.

Shukla, H.L., *Socio Caltural Approach to Trribal Languages*, D.K. Publishers Distributors (P) Ltd., New Delhi..

Shukla, H.L., *Tribal History: A New Interpretation*, B.R. Publishing Corporation, Delhi, 1988.

Shukla, H.L., *Socio Cultural Approach to Tribal Languages*, D.K. Publishers Distributors (P) Ltd., New Delhi..

Shukla, H.L., *Language: Ethicity and History*. Publishing Corporation, Delhi-7, 1985.

Shukla, H.L., *Dictinoary of Tribal Language : Historico-Comparative*: Hindi-English, B.R. Publishing Corporation, Delhi, 1987.

Shukla, B.K., *The Daflas of Subansiri Region, The People of NEFA Series*, Shillong, 1959.

Shyrock, Henry, et al, *The Methods and Materials of Demography* Vol. I, V.S. Bureau of Census, Washington D.C., 1971.

Shyamlal, *Education Among Tribals : Research Project on Tribal Education in Rajasthan*, D.K. Publishers Distributors (P) Ltd., New Delhi..

Siddigui, F.A., *Regional Analysis of Population Studies, A Study of Uttar Pradesh*, Concept Publishing Co., New Delhi. (India).

Simhadri, Y.C., *The Ex-Criminal Tribes of India*, National Publishing House, New Delhi-2, 1979.

Singh, Ajit Kumar, *Tribal Development in India*, Amar Prakashan Delhi, 1984.Singh Ajit Kumar, Tribal Development in India, Amar Prakashan Delhi, 1984.

Singh, Ajit Kumar, *Tribal Festivals of Bihar : A Functional Analysis*, D.K. Publishers Distributors (P) Ltd., New Delhi..

Singh, Bhupinder, *The Saora Highlander Leadership and Development*, D.K. Publishers Distributors (P) Ltd., New Delhi.

Singh, R.S., *Changing Occupational Structure of Schedule Tribes*, D.K. Publisher Distributors (P) Ltd. Delhi.

Singh, B.P., *The Problem of Change : A Study of North East India*, Delhi, Oxford University Press, 1987.

Singh, Ch Budhi, Fishing Economics of the Thanga, (A lake dwelling peasant Community cf Manipur, Unpublished Ph. D. thesis and now in Press) Gauhati Univ. 1972.

Singh, Chandrika, *Political Evolution of Nagaland*, Delhi, Learners Publishers, 1981.

Singh, D.P., *Culture Change in an Inter-Tribal Market*, Asia Publishing House, Bombay, 1968.

Singh, H. Bhuban, *The Merger of Manipur*, Pritam Haobam Gurukul Road, Lamphel-705004, Imphal.

Singh, K.B., The Meiteis of Manipur Valley, Unpublished Ph. D. Thesis, Bombay, Univ, 1964.

Singh, K.S., *Tribal Movements in India*, Vol. I & II Ramesh Jain, Monohar Publication, 2 Ansari Road, Daryanganj, New Delhi.

Singh, L. *Ibungohal, Introduction of Manipur*, Shri S. Babudhan Singh, Sagolband, Imphal, 1963.

Singh, L.M. *Ibungohal, An Introduction to Manipur*, Imphal, 1960.

Singh, M. Kirti, *Religious Development in Manipur in the Eighteenth and Ninteenth Centures*, Imphal. 1980.

Singh, Jumjao, *An Early History of Manipur*, 1966, Imphal.

Singh, N., Ibobi, *Manipur Adminstration*, 1976, Imphal.

Singh, O. Bhogeshwar, *Loina Shinlon*, Imphal, 1987, (Rept).

Singh, Pramod, *Problem of Wasteland and Forest Ecology of* India, Central N.S. (P) Ltd. 23/90, Connaught Circus, New Delhi, 1989.

Singh, R.K., Jhalajit, *A Short History of Manipur*, 1965, Imphal.

Singh, R.K., Sanahal, *Peeps into Manipur*, 1983, Imphal.

Singh, R.L., *India a Regional Grography*, National Grographical Society of India, Varanasi.

Singh, R.P.(1984) Manipur Hill Regional Study of a Tribal Habitat In: G.C. Toshi (ed). *Rural Development in Himalaya Problems & Prospects*, Gyanodaya Prakashan Nainaital.

Singh, R.P., *Grography of Manipur*, National Book Trust, India, New Delhi, 1982.

Singh, Rajendra, *The Annals of Manipur*, 1981.

Singh, Sanasam Gourahari, *Manipur and the Second World War* (in Verse) ,Nongmeikappam Biramani Singh, Chingamakha, Imphal.

Singh, Suresh Kumar, *Dust-Storm and Hanging Mist Study of Birsa Munda and His Movement*, K.L. Mukhopadhyaya, Calcutta, 1916.

Singh, V.R., *Land Use Pattern in Mirzapur and Environs*, Banaras Hindu University, Bananasi, India.

Singh, W., *Ibohal, A History of Manipur (Early Period)*, 1986 Imphal.

Singh, D.R., *Rural Leadership Among Scheduled Castes*, Delhi.

Singh, R.P., Manipur Hill Regional Study of A Tribal Habitat. In: G.C. Joshi (ed.). *Rural Development in Himalaya Problem and Prospects*, Gyanandyay Prakashan, Naintal, 1984.

Singh, Bhupinder & Bhandari, J.S, *The Tribal World and Its Transformation*, D.K. Publishers Distributors (P) Ltd. Delhi.

Sinha, S., (ed), *Tribal Politics and State System in Pre-Colonial Eastern and North Eastern India*, 1987.

Sinha, R., *The Akas of Shillong, Advisor's Secretariate*, NEFA, 1963.

Sinha, S.P., *Life and Times of Birsa Bhagwan*, Bihar Tribal Welfare Research Institute, Ranchi, 1964.

Sinha, S.P., *The Problem of Land Alienation of the Tribals in and around Ranchi*, Bihar Tribal Welfare Research Institute, Ranchi, 1968.

Sinha, R.R.P., *Tribal and Non-Tribal Intelegence*, D.K. Publishers Distributors (P) Ltd., New Delhi..

Sinha, A.C., *Studies in the Himalayan communities*, Text and Context, D.K. Publishers Distributors (P) Ltd., New Delhi..

Sinha, B.B., *Society in Tribal India*. D.K. Publishers Distributors (P) Ltd., New Delhi..

Sinha, Kamaleshwar, *Meghalaya, Triumph of the Tribal Genius*, Publication Division (ISSI) 3762, Netaji Subhash Road, Daryaganj, Delhi, 1970.

Srivasta, L.R.N., *The Gallong, Research Department Advisors*, Secretariat Shillong, 1962.

Shyamkanhai, Ksh. *Manipurgi Leingaklon Amasung Leingak Pathapki Itihas, 1762-1969*, Vol-I, Imphal. 1978.

Sonita, D.M., *Human Geography, A welfare approach Gulab Nazirani for Aenold,* Harinam Publisher, India, Pvt. Ltd. AB/ 9, Safdarzing Enclave, New Delhi-110029.

Smith, W.C., *The Ao Naga Tribes of Assam*, Macmillan & Co. Ltd. London, 1925.

Solanky, A.N., Dhodias of South Gujarat (M.A. Thesis) 1985.

Som, R.K., Demographic Factor in Planning for Economic and Social Development in African Countries, In: Ashish Bose et al (ed), *Studies in Demography*, George Allen & Unwin Ltd., London, 1970.

Soppitt, C.A., *An Historical and Descriptive Account of the Kachari Tribes in the North Cachar Hills with specimens of Tables & Folklore*, Shillong, 1885, Reptd. 190.

Soppitt, C.A., *A Short Account of the Kuki-Lushai Tribe on the North East Fronties Districts, Cachar, Sylhet, Naga Hills, North Cachar Hills etc.*, Shillong, 1887.

Spencer J.E. and Thomas, W.L., *Introducting Cultural Geography*, Secong Ed. John Willy & Sons, New York, Santa Barbara Chichestu, Brisbano, Toronto.

Spiro, Melford, E., *Kinship and Marriage in Burma*, Univ. of California Press, London, 1977.

Spochr, Florence Mann, *Among the Savages of the South Seas*, Stanford University Press Stanford, California, 1957.

Srivastava, S.K., *The Tharu: A Study in Cultural Dynamics*, Agra University Press, Agra, 1958.

Srivastava, S.K., (ed.), *Demographic Profile of North-East India*, 1987.

Srivastava, M.L. *Importance of Demography*, Demographic Research Centre, Patna, 1977.

Srinivasan, K., Saxena, P.C. Kanitkan, Tara (ed), *Demographic and Socio-Economic Aspects of the Child in India*, Himalaya Publishing House, Bombay, 1979.

Srinivasan, K. Roy, T.K. & Ghogate, S., Family Planning Targets by States for India : Under Alternative Programme Strategies to Reach Demographic goal of Net Reproduction, Rate of one. Monograph, Published by the IIPS, Bombay, 1980.

Srinivasan, K. and Mukerji, S. (ed), *Dynamic of Population and Population and Family Welfare*, Himalaya Publishing House and IIPS Bombay, 1981.

Srinivasan, K., Prospective Study of the Fertility Behaviour of a group of Married women in Rural India : Design and Findings of the First Round of Enquiry, *Population Review* July-Dec. 1967.

Srivastava, H.C., *Dependancy and Common Property Resources of Tribal Rural Poor*, Tripathi Book, Service, E, New Delhi-110005.

Stack E. and Lyall, C.J., *The Mikirs*, 1908

Sten, H.W., 1. *Meghalaya Year Book*, Shillong, 1971

Sten, H.W., 2. *Meghalaya Year Book*, Shillong. 1972

Sten, H.W., 3. *Meghalaya Year Book*, Shillong. 1973

Stracey, P.D., *Nagaland Nightmare*, Allied Publisher Pvt. Ltd. 15 Graham Road, Ballad Estate Bombay, 1, 1968.

Sujatha, K., *Education of the Forgotten Children of the Forests, (A case study of Yenadi Tribe)*, D.K. Publishers Distributors (P) Ltd., New Delhi.

Swinson, Arthur, *Kohima*, Cassell and Co. Ltd. 35 Red Lion Sequare, London WC, Melbouree, Sydeny, Toronto, Jonsburg, Cape Town Anchor, 1966.

Swanton, John R., *The Indian Tribes of North America*, Smithsonian Institution Press City of Washinton, 1952.

Talukdar, A.C., *Political Transition in the Grassroots in Tribal India* (North East India).

Taylor, Issac, *The Origin of the Aryans*, Bahri Publications Private Ltd. New Delhi. 1980 (1889).

Terwiel, B.J., *The Tai of Assam and Ancient Tai Ritual* in 2 Vols; Life-Cycle Ceremonies (Rep.) D.K. Publishers Distributors (P) Ltd., New Delhi.

Tewari, D.N., *Primitive Tribes of Madhya Pradesh : Strategy for Development*, Ministry of Home Affaris, New Delhi, 1984.

Thakur, Devendra, *Socio-Economic Development of Tribes in India*, D.K. Publishers Distributors (P) Ltd., New Delhi..

Thakur, G.C. Sharma, *The Tai Phakes of Assam*, B.R. Publishing Corporation, Delhi-52, 1982.

Thakur, R.N., *Himalayan Lepchad*, D.K. Publishers Distributors (P) Ltd., New Delhi., 1982.

Thakur, R.N., *Social Matrix of Tribal Village*, Central New Agency (P) Ltd. 23/90. Connaught Circus, New Delhi-110001, 1988.

Tanga, Lal Biak, *The Mizos*, United Publishers, Gauhati-1. 1978.

Thomas, M.M., et. al. *Tribal Awakening*, Bangalore, 1965.

Thurston, E., *Ethongraphic Notes in Southern India, Superintendent*, Madras Govt. Museum, madras, 1906.

Thurston, E., *Castes and Tribes of Southern India* (Vols.1 VII), Madras Govt. Press, madras, 1909.

Thusu, K.N., *The Dhurwa of Bastar*, Anthropological Survey of India, Calcutta, 1965.

Tippo, S., *Dynamics of Educational Development in Tribal India*, Classical Publications, New Delhi, 1979.

Tod, James, *Annals and Antiguities of Rajasthan*, (Crooks ed.) Oxford, 1920.

Todaro, Michael P., *Economics for a Developing World : As Introduction to Principle, Problems and Policies*, London Group Ltd. London, 1977.

Toppo, Sita, *Dynamics of Educational Development in Tribal India*, D.K. Publishers Distributors (P) Ltd. Delhi.

Trewartha, G.T., *Geography of Population : World Pattern*, New York, 1969.

Tripathy, R.N., *Technology Farm Output and Employment in a Tribal Region*, D.K. Publishers Distributors (P) Ltd., New Delhi..

Trivedi, H.V., *Economic Development of Tribes in India*, D.K. Publishers Distributors (P) Ltd., New Delhi..

Troisi, J., *The Santals a Classified and Aannotated Bibliography*, D.K. Publishers Distributors (P) Ltd., New Delhi..

Vanlawna, R., *Ka Ram Leh Kei* ("My Country and I"), Zoram Printing Press, Aijawl, 1972.

Vansina, Jan, *The Oral Tradition : A Study in Historical Methodology*, Chicago, Aldine-First Published in French. 1954 (1961).

Vasil, Ethnic *Politics in Malaysia.*

Verma, Maniklal, *Report of the All India Gaodia Lohar Convention*, All India Gadodia Lohar Seva Sangh, Chttorgarh, 1955.

Verma, K.K., Anthropo: Demogrpahy of the Santal and Birhor (Ph. D. Thesis, Ranchi Univ. University, Unpublished).

Verma, Y.M., *Problems of Tribal India*, D.K. Publishers Distributors (P) Ltd., New Delhi..

Vetch, Capt., *Report of Visit by Capt. Vetch to the Singhpo area and Naga Frontier in 1842*. Section of Selection of papers regarding the Hill Tracts between Assam and Barmah & on the Upper Brahmaputra, Calcutta, 1873.

Vidyarthi, L.P., *Tribal Culture of India*, K.P. Bagchi & Co. Calcutta, 1977.

Vidyarthi, L.P., *Cultural Contours of Tribal Bihar*, Punthi Pustak, Calcutta, 1964.

Vidyarthi, L.P., *Cultural Contours of Tribal Bihar*, Punthi Pustak, Calcutta, 1965b.

Vidyarthi, L.P., *Ghaghra: A Village of Tribal Bihar*, Census Operation, Delhi, 1965a.

Vidyarthi, L.P., *Industrialisation and Urbanisation in Tribal Area*: Paper Presented at the Indian Sociological Conference, Bombay, 1968.

Vidyarthi, L.P., *Socio-Cultural Implication of Industrialization in India; A Case Study of Tribal Bihar*, Research Programme Committee, Planning Commission, New Delhi, 1970.

Vidyarthi, L.P., *Study of Tribal Labourers of Both Industrial and Agricultural Areas in and around Ranchi*, National Commission on Labour, Manager of Publications, Delhi, 1968b.

Vidyarthi, L.P., *The Maler: A Study in Nature-Man-Spirit Complex of a Hill Tribe*, Bookland Pvt. Ltc. Calcutta, 1963.

Vidyarthi, L.P., *The Sacred Complex of Kashi*, Concept Publishing Co. Delhi-35. 1979.

Vidyarthi, L.P. (ed.) *Tribal Development and Its Administration*, Concept Publishing Co. New Delhi, 1986.

Vidyarthi, L.S. & Sahay, K.N. *The Dynamics of Tribal Leadership in Bihar*, Research Project on Changing Leadership in Tribal Society, 1967-1972, Kitab Mahal, Allahabab, 1976.

Vidyarthi, L.S. *The Dynamics of Tribal Leadership: in Bihar*, Research Project on Changing Leadership in Tribal Society 1977-1971. D.K. Publishers Distributors (P) Ltd., New Delhi.

Vyas, N.N. & R.S. Mann (ed.), *Indian Tribes in Transition*, Rawat Publications, Jaipur-Delhi-7, 1980

Vyas, N.N., *Bondage and Exploitation in Tribal India*, D.K. Publishers Distributors (P) Ltd., New Delhi..

Waddela, L.A. *The Tribes of the Brahmaputra Valley*. 1975 (1901). Sanskaran Prakashak, Delhi.

Wagner, Phillip L.& Mikesell, M.W., *Reading in Caltural Geography*, The University of Chicago Press, 1962.

Wati, *Imchaba Bendang, Eaducation Among the Nagas*, Illinois, 1949.

Watt, Neville A, *The Half Clad Tribals of Eastern India*, Oriental Longmans, Calcutta, 1978.

Wake, C. Staniland, *Serpent Worship and Other Easays With a Chapter on Totenism*, Londan, 1888.

Weling A., *The Katkaris: A sociological Study of a tribe of the Bombay Presidency*, Popular Book Depot, Bombay, 1984.

Whitehead, George, *In the Nicobar Island*, London, 1924.

Woodthorpe, R.G., *The Lushai Expedition*, 1871-1872, Spectrum Publications, Gauhati.

Zatluanga, *Mizo Chanchin*, Khuma Printing Press, Aizawl.1966.

Zelinsky, W., *A Prologue to Population Geography*, Prentice-Hall of India (Pvt. Ltd.) New Delhi, 1966.

ARTICLES

Aslok, S.W., "The Morang organisation among the Nokte Nagas, *Vanyajati*, 1956, 4(2, 73-78).

Abelson, A.E. T.S. Baker and P.T. Baker, "Altitude Migration and Fertility in the Andes" *Social Biology*, 1974, 21, 12-29.

Agarwal, H.N., "Reproductive Life of Onge Women", *Vanyajati*, 15, 1967.

Agarwal, B.N., "The North Eastern Council and Self Reliance" *North Eastern Spectrum*, Vol. II, March-May, 1978, No. 9-11, pp. 17-20.

Aiyappan, A., "Urgent Anthropology for Southern India, in Beharilal Abbi and Satish Sabarwal (eds.) *Urgent Research in Social Anthropology*, India Institute of Advanced Study, Simla, 1969, 34-40.

Aiyappan, A., "Social and Physical Aanthropology of the Nayadis of Malabar", Bullentin of the Madras, Govt. Museum, 1937, 2(4).

Aiyappan, A., Handmande Pottery of the Urali Kurumbars of Wyand, S. India",*Man*, 1947, 47 (54).

Aiyappan, A., Iravas and Culture Change", Bulletin of Madras Govt. Museum, General Section, 1944, 5(1), 1-204.

Ali, S.A., "Incidence of Crime Among the Tribes of Madhya Pradesh", in Vidhyarthi (ed.), *Applied Anthropology in India*, Kitab Mahal, Allahabad, 1968.

Ali, S., and Ripley, D.S., "The Birds of Mishmi Hills", *J. Bombay Nat. Hist. Soc.*, Vol. XLVIII, 1948, pp. 1-37.

Anal, Johnson, "A Brief History of the Anal People", Presented in the Seminar on the History of Manipur, Centre for Post Graduate Studies in History, Jawaharlal Nehru University, 1975.

Anon, A Female Mowgli Found in the Jungle of Naintal" Folklore, (London), 1916, 27, 418-19.

Anon, "Baiga Poetry", *Man in India*, 1943, 23.

Anon, "Festival Songs", *Man in India*, 1943a, 24.

Anon, "More Santal Songs", *Man in India*, 1944b. 24.

Anon, "Traditional Arts and Crafts in Tripura, Manipur and Assam", Bulletin of the Institute for Traditional Culture, (Madras), 1957, pp. 200-205.

Ao, P. Shilee, "Report of the Study on Tribal Development programmes (All India)", Committee on Plan Projects, Planning Commission, New Delhi, 1969.

Ao, Temsula, "The culture of Nagas" *North Eastern Spectrum*, Vol. I, Dec. 1976, No. 6, P. 49-54.

Apte, B.K., "The Maratha Weapons of War", Bulletin of the Decan College Research Institute, 1958, 19 (1 and 2), 106-124.

Archer, W.G. and Prasad, S., "More Santal Songs", *Man in India*, 1944b, 24 141-144.

Ashali, N., "The Customes and Tradition of the Hill People of Manipur-The Mao Nagas", Paper Presented at Seminar held at Imphal, 29-30, Nov.1972.

Bailey, F.G., An Oriya Hill Village: in M.N. Srinvias (ed.) India's Villages,. Asia Publishing House, Bombay, 1955.

Bailey, F.G., An Oriya Hill Village II, in M.N. Srinivas (ed). *India's Villages*, Asia Publishing House Bombay, 1955b.

Bailey, F.M., Journey through a Portion of South-Eastern Tibet and the Mishmi Hills, *Geographical Journal*, Vol. XXXIX (1912), pp. 334-471.

Binbridge, R.B., The Saorias of the Rajmahal Hills, *Memoirs of the Asiatic Society of Bengal*, 1907, 26, 43-64.

Balaratnam, L.K., Serpent Worship in Kerala, *Man in India*, 1946, 26(1) 53-64.

Balfour, H., Asiatic Origin of the Reflexed 'Horn Bow' *Journal of the Royal Anthropological Institute*, 1921.

Balfour, H., Some Types of Native Hou, Naga Hills, *Man*, 1917, 17 (74).

Balfour, H., Thorn-Lived and their Distributor, *Man* (March, 1925), Goves examples of change and Sangtam teaps.

Bandopadhyay, Hira Biswanath, Potters of Assam, *Man in India*, 1961; 41(1), 25-44.

Banerjee, Sukumar, Impact of Industrialization on the Tribal Population of Rangunge Coalfield area, *Journal of the Indian Anthropological Society*, 1982, 17 (2), 193.

Banarjee, Gopa, "A Note on the Dancing Girl (Nachni) of Purulia", *Man in India*, LIII, 1973, 3, 279-293.

Banarjee, Sukumar, "Phar Kinship System", *Bulletin of the Anthropolotical Survey of India*, 1964, 13 (1-2).

Banarjee, Sukumar, "Residence Pattern Among the Phar", *Bulletin of the Anthropological Survey of India*, 1964, 13 (1-2), 106-110.

Banerjee, S.K., "Role of Handicraft in Tribal Economic", *Bulletin of Cultural Research Institute* 1963, 1(3), 15-19.

Banerji, Adris, "Phulkaris: A Folk Art of Punjab", *Marg*, 1954-55, 8(3), 59-64.

Bapat, N.V.M., "A Few Thoughts on Tribal Education", *Vanyajati*, 1964, 12 (4), 190-194.

Bapat, N.V.M., "Tribal Education on Problems", *Vanyajati*, 1961, 2 (1), 37-39.

Bareh, H. "Meghalaya: Glimpses From Her Ancient History", *North-Eastren Spectrum*, Vol. I, Dec. 1976, No. 6, 13-19.

Barnes, "The Bhils of Western India", Journal of Asiatic Society of Arts, 1907, 55, 324-336.

Barnes, J.A., "Class and Committees in a Norwegian Island Parist", *Human Relations*, 1954, 7 (1), 39-59.

Barpujari, S.K., "Early Peace Mission to the Naga Hills", *Indian History Congress*, P. 369-375

Barpujari, S.K., "Naga Hills Boundary Disputes 1842-72" *Journal of Indian History*, Vol II Part II, Aug. 1973, Serial No.152. 271-280.

Barua, A., "Beginning of Freedom Movement in Assam" *North-Eastern Spectrum*, Vol. I, May-June, 1977, Nos.11-12.

Barua, A., "The Ahom Rules and the Neighbouring Tribes" *North Eastren Spectrum*, Vol.I, Sept.- Oct. 1976. Nos. 3 and 4, 16-18.

Barua, B.P. "Status of Hill Tippera as a Native" State" *Journal of Indian History*, Vol.II Part II, 1973, Serial No. 152, 129-335.

Baruah, S.L., "Ahom Policy Towards the Neighbouring Hill Tribes", *Indian History Congress*, 38th Session, Utkal University, Bhubaneswar (1977) P. 249- 256.

Baden Powell, B.H. "Notes on the Origin of 'Lunar' and 'Solar' Aryan Tribes and on the Royal Asiatic Society of Great Britian and Ireland, 1899, 31, 295- 328, 519-563.

Badgley, W.F., "Extract from the Narrative Report of Captain W.F. Badgley" General Report on the Topograhphical Servey of India for the Season 1874-5 (Calcutta, 1876), Gives some account of the Wanchos.

Badgley, W.F., Report on the Treacherous Attack made by the Nagas, General Report on the Topographical Surveys of India for the Season 1874-5 (Calcutta, 1876) Describes the massacre of a Survey Party by the Chos of Nine.

Badgley, W.E., "The Lushais", *Indian Antiguary*, 2, 1873.

Basu, Arabinda, "A Demographic Study of the Kota of Nilgiri Hills", *Journal of the Indian Anthropological Society*, 1972, 7, 29-45.S

Basu, Arabinda, "Selection Intensity in the Paniras" *Eugenlls Quarterly*, 1967, 1967, 14, 221-242.

Basu, Arabinda, "The Pahira : A Population Gennetic Study", *American Journal of Physical Anthropology*, 1969, 31, 399-416.

Basu, M.N., "Anthropology in Tribal Education", *Bulletin of the Cultural Research Insitute*, 1963, 2(1), 22-27.

Basu, M.N., "A Munda Colony in Bengal" *Journal of the Department of Letters*, University of Calcutta, 1935, 27, 1-4.

Basu, M.N., "Bunas of Bengal", *Journal of the Department of Letters*, University of Calcutta, 1939, 32, 1-120.

Basu, M.N., "Ethnic Anlysis of the Koms of Manipur" *Indian Science Congress*, 1936.

Basu, M.N., "Suggestions for the Educational Plan of the Aboriginal People of India", *Vanyajati*, 1961, 9(3), 123-126.

Basu, M.N., "The Koms of Manipur", *Calcutta Review*, 1939.

Basu, P.C., "Head-Dress of the Hill Tribes of Assam", *J.R.A.S.S.*, Vol. XXV (N.S. 1929).pp. 103-104.

Bebanta, Prafulla C., "Family Type and Fertility – A Case Study in Six Indian Villages", *Economic and Political Weekly*, (17) 19, 1966.

Behura, N.K., "Santal Sub-nationalism and New Identity the orissa Situations", *Journal of the Indian Anthropological Society*, 1981, 16 (2), 131-144.

Bentinek, A., "The Abor Expedition: Geographical Results", *Grographical Journal*, Vol. XLI (1913), pp. 613-18.

Beierwltos W.H. and Taman J., "Epindemic Goitre and Cetinism in Michigan and in the North-Eastern Forntier Agency Area", *Current Medical Practice*, Vol. I, No. 11 (1957). Pp. 613-18.

Berreman, G.D., "Cultural Varibility and Drift in the Himalayan Hills", *American Anthroplogist*, 1960. 62(5), 774-794.

Berreman, G.D., "Urgent Anthropology in India", in Beharilal Abbi and Satish Sabarwal (eds.) Urgent Researches in Social Anthropology, Indian Institute of Advanced Study. Simla, 1969.

Betts, U., "The Village duel in Apatani Society", *Man in India*, Vol XXVIII (1948), pp. 163-9.

Betts, U., "The Daflas of the Subansiri Area", *R.Cent Asian Journal*, Vol. XXXVI (1949), pp. 146-54.

Bhadra, Gautam, "The Kuki Upsiring (1917-1919) its Causes and Nature", *Man in India*, Vol. 55. 1975, p.14.

Bhaduri, M.B., "Hindu Influence on Munda Songs" *Essays on Anthropology present to S.C. Roy*, Calcutta, 1942, 156-26.

Bhagbati, Ananda, "Anthropological Researches in Assam Region", in Beharilal Abbi and Satish Sabarwal (eds.) Urgent Researches in Social Anthropology, Indian Institute of Advanced Study, Simla, 1969, 54-60.

Bhagabati, A.C. and Bibhash Dhar, "Tribesemen as Townmen: A Case Study in Assam", *Bulletin of the Dept. of Anthropology*, Dibrugarh University, 1976, 5, 62-70.

Bhagabati, A.C., "Some Aspects of Emergent Tribal Identity in North-East India", *The Bulletin of the Anthropology*, Dibrugarh University, 198.7 and 8.

Bhagwat Burga, Baradeo "The High God of the Gonds", *Journal of the Anthropological Society of Bombay*, 1953, 7, 60-71.

Bhagwat Durga, "The Sparrow and the Cow, *Indian Folklore*, 1959, 1, 213-15.

Bhale, Vaijanti "Differentical Fertility" *Artha Vijnna*, (5)3, 1961.

Bhattarcharjee, J.B., "Early British Policy in North East India: Garo hills 1765-1792", *North-Eastern spectrum*, Vol. 1, Dec., 1976, No. 6. 13-14.

Bhattarcharjee, J.B., "Early History of Education in Garo Hills" *Shodhak*, Vol. 3, et. A, Jaipur, 1974.

Bhattarcharjee, J.B., "Justice and Police in Garo-Hills 1826-1874" University Law College Mazaine, Gauhati University, 1971.

Bhattarcharjee, J.B., "Marriage:Integrating Institution in Garo Society", *Journal of North East India Council for Social Science Research*, Shillong, 1977.

Bhattarcharjee, J.B., "Pattern of British Administration in the Garoland", *Journal of Indian History*, Vol. LI, Pt. III, Trivandrum, 1973.

Bhattarcharjee, J.B., "Problem of Garo-Frontier Defence" proceedings, *Indian History Ccongress*, 1972

Bhattarcharjee, J.B., "Problem of Mymensing-Rangpur Frontier Defence, 1765-1826", *Quarterly Review of Histroical Studies*, Vol. XIV, No. 4, Calcutta, 1975.

Bhattarcharjee, J.B., "Progress of Education in Garo Hills" 1826-1874", Proceedings, *Indian History Congress*, 1970.

Bhattarcharjee, J.B., "The Garos under the Zamindars, 1775 to 1816", Proceedings, *Indian History Congress*, 1969.

Bhattarcharjee, J.B., "The Genesis and Pattern of British Administration in the Hill Areas of North East India", Proceedings, *Indian History Congress*, 1970.

Bhattacharjee, J.B., "A Note on the Mughal Policy Towards the Garos", Proceedings, *Indian History Congress*, 1970.

Bhattacharjee, P.N., "Sero-genetical Study of the Khasi and Their genetical relationship", *The Eastern Anthropologists*, 1975. 28, 171-177.

Bhattacharya, A.N., "Effect of Tribal and Caste Factor on Rural Settlement in U.P., *Indian Geographical Journal*, 1956, 31(39).

Bhattacharya, A., "The Plain Tribals Movement in Assam" *People's Democaracy*, June, 23, 1968, P.11.

Bhattacharya, A., "The Tribal Question Again", *People's Democracy*

(Delhi), June, 9, 1968, P.3.

Bhattacharya, B.K., "A Glimpse of Tangkhul Life", *New Voice*, '956, 1(2), 25-28.

Bhattacharya, B.K., "A Glimpse of Manipur", *North-Eastern Spectrum*, Vol. I, July, 1976, No. 1, 63-65.

Bhattacharya, B.K., "Cachar in History", *North Eastern Spectrum*, Vol. II, March-May, 1978, No. 9-11, 31-34.

Bhattacharya, P.N., "A General Study of the Santals of Santal Pargana", *The Anthropologist*, 1969, Special Volume, 98-103.

Bhattacharya, P.N., "Dematoglyphic of the Abor People in Assam", *The Anthropologist*, Vol. 11. No. 2 (1955).

Bhattacharya, S.B., "The Munda Language in Ancient India" *Journal of Indian History*, Vol. II. April, August, 1977, part I and II, p. 25-33.

Bhowmic, P.K., "Approach to Tribal Welfare" *Bulletin of the Dept. of Anthropology*, Dibrugarh University, 1978-79. 7 and 8, 142-159.

Bhowmic, P.K., "The Lodha : Denotified Community of West Bengal", *Man in India*, Vol. 63, No. 3 September 1983, pp. 223-248.

Bhutani, V.C., "The Study of North-East Frontier of India and Its Sources: The Significants of Assam Archives", *Indian History Congress*, 38th Session, Utkal University (Bhuvaneswar), 1977, pp. 595-602.

Biswas, A.K. and Muller, M.G., "Population Growth and economic Development of India", AICC, *Economic Review*, 15 November. 1955.

Biswas, P.C., "Anthropology and Tribal Education", *Vanyajati*, 1965, 3(2), 81-83.

Biswas, P.C., "A Short Note on the Limbus of Darjeeling", *Indian Culture*, 1934-1935, b,1. 481-482.

Biswas, P.C., "Lepchas of Sikkim", *Indian Culture, Indian Culture*, 1934-35a, 1.483-486.

Biswas, P.C., "Tribal Education", (Report of the symposium on Problems of Education of the Tribal People of India, N.C.E.R.T., Delhi, 1966, 3-5.

Biswas, P.C., The Utility of Research for the Tribal People", *Vanyajati*, 1964, (1) 8-9.

Bodding, P.O., "Traditions and Institutions of Santals", Oslo, Ethnographic Museum, 1942, Bulletin 6.

Bonnerjee, Biren, "Ugrian Fishing Implements and Some Indian Parallels", *Man in India*, 1938, 18, 225-263.

Bore, N.L., "The Daflas and Their Oaths", *J.R.A.S.B.* Vol. II (Third Series, 1936), pp-27-39.

Bose, Ashish, "Why do People Migrate to City"?, *Yojana* 26 January 1965.

Bose, J.K., "Dual Organization in Assam", *Journal of the Dept. of Letters*, University of Calcutta, Vol. XXV (1) 1939a (1-29).

Bose, J.K., "Ethnic Position of the Marings of Manipur, Assam", *Man and Life*, 1982, 8 (3 and 4).

Bose, J.K., "Garo Laws of Inheritance" Anthropological papers, University of Calcutta, 1941 (6) 81-150.

Bose, J.K., "Marriage Classes Among Tarao Kukis of Assam", 24th *Indian Science Congress*, Hyderabad, 1937.

Bose, J.K., "Marriage Classes Among the Chirus of Assam" *Man*, Vol. XXXVII, No. 189. pp. 160-2, 1937.

Bose, J.K., "Notes on the Kabuis of Manipur", Current Sc. 1934, 2.

Bose, J.K., "Social Organization of the Aimol Kukis", *Journal of the Dept. of Letters*, University of Calcutta, Vol. XX, pp. 1-9. 1934b.

Bose, J.K., "The Chothe Kukis of Manipur", Current Science, 1934, 2.

Bose, J.K., The Gana Mokna Ceremony of the Garos of Assam" *Man in India*, 19, 38, 18 (283), 168-173.

Bose, J.K., "The Nokrom System of the Garos of Assam", *Man*, 1936, Vol XXXVI, No.54. pp.44-6, 1936.

Bose, N.K., "Hindus Method of Tribal Assorption", Proceedings of the *Indian Science Congress* (Reprinted in Cultural Anthropology), Calcutta, 1941.

Bose, N.K., "Juang Association", *Man in India*, 1929, 9 (1), 47-53.

Bose, N.K., "Marriage and Kinship Among the Juangs", *Man in India*, 1928, 8(4), 233-242.

Bose, N.K., "National Seminar on Hill People", *Man in India*, 1967, 47(1).

Bose, J.K., "The Religion of Aimol Kukis", *Man in India*, Vol. 14, 1934, p.1.

Brown, R., "Annual Report on the Munnipore Political Agency for 1868-9", Selections from the Records of the govt. of India, No. LXXVIII, Calcutta, 1874.

Bose, S., "Carrying Capacity of Land under Shifting Cultivation, The Asiatic Society Monograh Series, XII, Calcutta, 1967.

Bose, S., "Economy of The Onge of Little Andaman", *Man in India*, ,1964, 44.

Bose, S., "Impact of Changing Conditions on the Economy of the High Attitude People (Read in a Seminar on Tribal Situation in India, Indian Institute of Advanced Study, Simla), 1969.

Bose, S., "The Bhot of Northern Sikkim", *Man in India*, 1966, 46 (2), 166-171.

Bose, S., "The Gaddi of Chamba", *Man in India*, 1963, 43(3), 191, 213.

Bose, S., "Land use Survey in a Juang Village", *Man in India*, 1961, 41 (3), 172-183.

Bower, U., "The Kabui and Tangkhul nagas", Royal Central Asian Journal, Vol. XXVI, 1939, pp. 5-19.

Buchi, E.C., "Onge of Little Andaman", in Tribal People India, Govt. of India, Delhi, 1955.

Budhi Singh, Ch. "Ethnographic Note on the Purum (Chothe) Presented in Symposium on Tribal Demography in India, Sponsored by India Association for the study of Population and Jawaharlal Nehru University, 1976.

Burman, M.D., "Our Indigenenous Peoples-Tribals of Tripura, Autonomy is the only Situation", Resistance: July 12, 1977, pp.3-4.

Burman, M.D., "Our Indigenenous Peoples-Tribals of Tripura, Autonomy is the only Situation", Resistance: July 16, 1977, pp.3-4.

Butta, J., "A Rough Comparative Vocabulary of Sub More Language", *Journal of the Asiatic Society of Bengal*, Vol. XLXI pt. 1, App. 1 (1873), pp. 2-29.

Butler John, "Rough Notes on the Angami Naga and Their Language", Journal of Asiatic Society of Bengal, 1857, 44 (Part I), 307-346.

Cammiade, L.A., " Ironsmelting by Kois, A Jungle Tribe in the Eastern Ghats of India", *Man*, 1931, 31 (65).

Campbell, A., "The Losshais", Journal of Royal Anthropological Insitute of Great Britian and Inreland, 1874.3

Cambell, J.M., "Ethnography of India", Journal of Asiatic Society of Bengal, 1856, 35.

Carstairs, G.M., "The Bhils of Kotra Bhoma", *Eastern Anthropologist*, 1953-54, 7, 169-181.

Carstairs, G.M., "A Village in Rajasthan : A Study in Rapid Social Change", Economic Weekly, 1952a, 4, 75-77.

Carstairs, G.M., "Bhill Villages of Western Udiapur: A Study in Resistance to Social change", Economic Weekly, 1952b, 4, 231-233.

Cawley, Mrs., "Account of the Seize of Kohima in 1879", Assam Review, May, 1930.

Chakladar, H.C. and T.C. "The Kabui : A Naga Group of Manipur", *Man in India*, Roy Choudhury, 1957, 37 (3).

Chakrabarti Mukul, "A B O Blood Groups of Zeliang Naga", *Man in India*, Vol. 45, 1965, p. 34.

Chakraborty, R. and S. Yee, "Phenolypic bioassay of five Tribes of Orissa", *Human Heredity*, 1973, 23, 270-279.

Chandrasekhar, S., "Cultural Bareriers to Family Planning in Underdeveloped Countries", *Population Review*, I, 1957.

Chandrasekhar, C., "Fertility Trends and National Policy", *Journal of Family Welfare*, 10.3.1964.

Chandasekhar, S., "Population Growth in Relation to Economic Development, *Nutrition as a Centraceptive Population Review*, 1970.

Chandasekhar, C., "Indian Fertitlity in a Changing Ecinomic and Social Setting", *Family Planning News*, 13 (10), 1962.

Chatterji, B.K. and G.D. Kumar, "The Somantic Character and Their Recial Affinities" G.D. Kumar Asiatic Society, 1952, 18, 72d-82.

Chatterji, B.K. and G.D. Kumar, "Hunting and Fishing Appliances of the Onges of Little Andaman and their Affinities with Negrito Races", *Vanyajati*, 1954. 2, 79-82.

Chatterji, S.K., "Purana Apocrypha: A Manipura-Purana", In E. Bender (ed.), Indological Studies in Honour of W. Norman Brown, (American Oriental Series, 47) : 28-41. 1962, New Heaven.

Chattopadhyay, K.P., "Tribal Education", *Man in India*, 1953, 23 (1), 1-18.

Chattopadhyay, K.P., "How Korkus Live", Journal of the Asiatic society, 1957, 22(2), 99-137.

Chattopadhyay, K.P., "A Torsion Trap of Korkus, *Vanyajati*, 1955b, 3, 58-59.

Chattopadhyay, K.P., "A Santal Trap", Journal of the Asiatic Society, 1955a, 21, 29-30.

Chattopadhyay, K.P., "The Bondon Tree Press and Its Links", *Journal of the Asiatic Society of Bengal* 1958, 24 (2), 7-12.

Chattopadhyay, K.P., "An Essay on the History of Newar Culture", Journal and Proceeding of Asiatic Society of Bengal, 1925, 8(3).

Chattopadhyay, K.P., "Some Malayalam Kinship Terms", *Man in India*, 1922, 2(2).

Chattopadhyay, K.P., "Khasi Land Ownership and Scale", *Eastern Anthropologist*, 1949, 2, 115-124.

Chaudhuri, S.S. Dutta, "Demographic Profile of Miji (Sajolang) of Arunachal Pradesh, man in India, 1988, 68(4), 442-447.

Chaudhuri, Mamata, "Ancient Indian Tribes and their Intergration into the Hindus Society" *Jourciety*, 1976, 2(2), 125-145.

Chauhan, Indira, "Tribal Development Administration in Madhya Pradesh", *Eastern Anthropologist*, 1988, 41 (1), 87-92.

Chauhan, Brij Raj, "Tribalization in Tribe", *Journal of the Rajasthan Tribal Research Institute*, Udaipur, Vol. 1, No. 1, 1964.

Chengapa, B.S., "On the Shom Pen of Great Nicobar", Census of India, 1951, 17. (The Andaman and Nicobar Islands).

Chhiller, R.S. and Gurcharan Singh, "Animal Husbandary in Tribal Areas", *Kurukshetra*, July 16-31, 1977.

Choudhury, N.C., "Cultural Types and Level of Indian Tribal Societies: The Tribes of chotanagpur", *Proceedings of Summer School in Anthropology, Darjeeling Anthropological Survey of India*, Calcutta, 1966.

Choudhury, N.C., "The Problems of Development of Small Tribes", in Buddhadeb Chaudhuri (ed.) *Tribal Development in India*, 1982.

Choudhury, A.K., "PTC Taste Sensitivity and Colour-Blindness among the Bodh and Swangla of Lahaul (Himachal Pradesh", *Man in India*, 1988, 68(4), 448-453.

Choudhury, Dilip., "An Analitical Study of Students", Unrest" *North Eastern Spectrum*, Vol. II, September October., 1977, No. 3-4.pp. 12-13.

Cipriani, Lidio, "Survey of Little Andaman During 1954 Bulletin of the dept. of Anthropology 1966, 2 (2), 1954.

Clark, E.W., "A Specimen of the Zoongee (or Zurngee Dialect of the Tribe of Nagas, Bordering on the valley of Assam, between the Dikho and Desoi Rivers, embracing over 40 villages", *Journal of the Royal Asiatic Society*, Vol. II, (N.S. 1879). Pp. 278-86.

Clark, E., "The sociological Significance of Ancestor-Worship in Ashanti", *Africa*, Vol. III, pp. 431-70. 1930.

Cole, W.H.G., "Ethnographic Notes: The Lushais", Census of India, 1911, 3 Govt. Secretariat Press Shillong, 1912.

Conklin, H.C., "Hanunoo Agriculture: A Report on an Integral System of Shifting Cultivation in the Philipines", FAO Foeestry Department Paper, 1957, 12, XII, 209.

Coomaraswasny, Anand K., "The Blow Pipe in Persa and India", *American Anthropologist*, 1943, 45,

Crooke, W., "Karma Jhumata: A Hunting Song of Korwar on the Chotanagpur border", *North Indian Notes and Queries*, 1891, 1. 159-160.

Crooke, W., "Note on the Art Industries of Mirzapur", *Journal of Indian Art and Industry*, 1893, 5(44). 55-56.

Crooke, W., "Songs Sung by Kols During the Sacred Dance of the Karma", *North Indian Notes and Queries*, 1892, 2. 92-128.

Culshaw, W.J., "The Santals of West Bengal", *Man*, 1947, 47 (103).

Cutting, C.S., "Jungle People of Assam, Customs and Ceremonies of the Nagas", *Natural History*, Vol. LXXXIII. 1938, pp. 54-65.

Damant, G.H., "The Two Brothers: A Manipur Story", *Indian Antiquary*, 4 : 260-64, 1875.

Damant, G.H., "Contribution to the Ethography and Histroy of Manipur", *Journal of the Asiatic Society of Bengal*, 1877, 27.

Damant, G.H., "Notes on the Old Manipuri Characters", *Journal of the Asiatic Society of Bengal*, 1877, XXVI-I.

Damant, G.H., "Notes on the Locality and Population of the Tribes Dwelling Between Brahmaputra and Ningthi rivers", *Journal of the Royal Asiatic Society of Bengal*, 1877, XXVI-1. Vol. XII (N.S. 1880), pp.228-58.

Danda, Ajit K., "Ethnic Status, Identity and Heerarchy : the Purum Case", *Journal of the Indian Anthropological Society*, 1987, 22 (1), 52-64.

Danda, Ajit K., "Tribals in India", *Man in India*, 1988, 68 (4), 313-334.

Danda, Ajit K., "Santal Tree Press" (Correspondence), *Science and Culture*, 1963, 29(3), 155.

Danda, Dipali, "The Semsa Economy", *Journal of Indian Anthropological Society*, 1981, 16(2), 95-106.

Das, A., "The Santals – A Glimpse into their Life and Activities", Seminar on Development Aspects of Tribal Areas, (Unpublished), Bhubaneswar, 1980.

Das, A.K., "Influence of City Life on Educated Tribals", *Bulletin of Cultural Research Institute*, 1962, 1(2), 69-78.

Das, A.K., "Special Problems on Tribal Transformation : Industrialisation as Mens of such Transformation", *Bulletin of the Cultural Research Institute*, Calcutta, 1966, 5(1 and 2).

Das, B.M and R. Das, "A Study of the Mikir foot", *Journal of the Gauhati University*, 1968, XVI-XVIII,No 2.

Das, B.M., "A Study on the Planner Prints of the Khasi of Assam", Proceedings of Internaltional Symposium on Dermatoglyphic, ed. By P.C.Biswas and A. Sharma, Dept. of Anthropology, Delhi University.1968.

Das, M.N., "Female Infanticide Among the Khond of Orissa", *Man in India*, 1969, 40(1), 30-35.

Das, N., "Tribal Integration of the Saoras and Paros of Ganjam Agency", *Adivasi*, 1967-68a, 12 and 13.

Das, N.K., "Review of the Works on Social Structures of some Matrilineal Tribes of North-East India and observations thereon", *Journal of the Indian Anthropological Society*, 1982, 17 (3), 199-214.

Das, R. and B.M. Das., "A Study of the Hira foot", *Man in India*, 1967, 47(2).

Das, R.K., "Marriage and Kinship among the Kabui Nagas of Manipur" *Man in India*, 1972, 52(3).

Das, R.K. and R.K. Ranjit Singh, "A New Socio-Political Identity among the Loi-A Scheduled Casetė of Manipur", *Journal of the Indian Anthropological Society*, 1976. 11(2).

Das, R.K., "Our Indigenour Peoples – The Marings", *Resistance*: March 1, 1977, pp. 3-4,

Das, R.K., "Our Indigenour Peoples – The Marings", *Resistance*: March 8, 1977, pp.3-4.

Das, R.K., "Our Indigenour Peoples – The Marings", *Resistance*: March 15, 1977,pp.3.

Das, R.K., "Trends of Change among the Tribes of Manipur" Regional Integration, Imphal, 1976, 19 (7).

Das, R.K., "The Effect of New Methods of Productivity on a Maring Village" in Cultural and Physical Adaptation in North East India, A Seminar Volume Published by the Dept. of Anthropology, Dibrugarh Universty, 1978.

Das, Rajat Kanti, "Problem and Prospects in the Study of Tribal groups in Manipur", *Journal of the Indian Anthropological Society*, 1987.22 (2-3).

Das, R.K., "Some Aspects of Changing Social Relations: A Study of a Thadiou Village", Journal of Social Research, 1979, 22 (1).

Das, R.K., "The Maring: A Frontier Tribe of Manipur", ICSSR Research Abdtracts Quarterly, 1980, 19 (1-2).

Das, R.K., "An Analysis of the Maring Consaguined Kin Group", *Journal of the Indian Anthropological Society*, 1981, 16.

Das, R.K., "Observation, In Purum (Chothe) Revisted", Anthropological Survey of India, Calcutta, 1985.

Das, R.K., "The Problems of Tribal Identity in Manipur'. *Eastren Anthropologist*, 1971, 24 (2).

Das, R.K. and L.R. "Koirengei Haotabi- A Kabui Naga Village in Manipur", *Eastern Anthropologist*, Lucknow, 1968, 21 (1).

Das, R.K., "Rituals in Maring Social Life", *Man and Life*, 1982, 8 (1and2).

Das, R.K., "Immigration and Demographic Transformation of Assam 1891- 1981', *Economic and Political Weekly*, May 10, 1980, pp. 856-58.

Das, T.C., "Aspects of Tribal Vulture Under Modern Impact in Eastern India", in Bala Ratnam (ed.), *Anthropology on the March*, Social Science Association, Madras, 1963 , 137-154.

Das, T.C., "A Scheme for Tribal Welfare", in Vidyarthi (ed.), *Applied Anthropology in India*, Kitab Mahal, Allahabad, 1968.

Das, T.C., "The Wild Kharias of Dhalbhum", *Anthropological Papers*, University of Calcutta, 1931a, 3.

Das, T.C., "The Chirus of Manipur –Their Descent and Social Organisation of the Purum Kukis of Manipur" *Journal of the Dept. of Leters*, Calcutta University, 1935, 38.

Das, T.C., "Some Notes on the Economic and Agricultural Life of a little Know Tribe on the Eastern Frontier of India" *Anthropos*, 1937.32.

Das,T.C., Clan Monopoly of Personal Names among Purum Kudis", *Man*, 1939, 39.

Das,T.C., "The Purums: An Old Kuki Tribe of Manipur" *Anthropological Papers* (NS), 1941, 6. Calcutta University.

Das, Swapan K., Partha P. Majumdar and Amitasbha Basu, "Demorgaphy and Demographical Genetics of two Isolated Mountain Villages of Northern Sikkim, Eastern Himalayas", *Journal of the Anthropological Society*, 1982, 17(2), 155-162.

Das Gupta, B.K., "Present Day Purum (Chothe) Society with Special Reference to Marriage Alliance", In Purum (Chote) Revisited, Anthropological Survey of India, Calcutta, 1985.

Dasgupta, Biman Kumar, "Social Mobility Movement Among the Tribes of Eastern Central India", *Journal of the Indian Anthropological Society*, 1978, 13(1).

Dasgupta, Biman Kumar, "A Short Note on Khasi Smithery", *Man in India*, 1963a. 43(3), 353-354.

Dasgupta, Biman Kumar, "Pot Making in and Around Tinsukia. District Lakhimpur, Assam" Bullentin of Anthropological Survey of India, 1963b. 12(1-2).

Dasgupta, Biman Kumar, and Shyam Choudhury, N.K., "ACultural Survey of Indigrnous Earthen Ware in the Khasi and Jaintia Hills", *Bulletin of Anthropological Survey of India*, 1962, 11.

Das Gupta and P. Chandra, "A Note on the Kom People of Manipur", Journal of the Dept. of Letters, Calcutta University, 1935, 27.

Datta, B.N., "Traces of Totemism in Some Tribes of North-Eastern India", *Man in India*, Vol. 13, 1933, p. 97.

Datta, Birendra Nath, "Re-Emergence of Floklore: The North-East India Scene", *Man and Life*, Vol. 11, Nos. 1 and 2, January-June, 1985, pp.77-87.

Datta Chaudhuri, S.S. and Dhar, B., "Tribes in Contemporary India: Miji of West Kameng", of Traditional Culture", (Unpub.).

Davidson, D.S., "Family Hunting Territory of Australia", *American Anthropologist*, Vol. XXX, P. 614-31, 1928a.

Davis, H. and Warner, W.L., "Structural Analysis of Kinship", *American Anthropologist*, Vol. XXXVII, pp. 291-313, 1935.

Deka, Ranjan, "Selecion Potential Among the Sonowal Kachari of Upper Assam", *Bulletin of the Dept. of Anthropology*, Disbrugarh University 1980, 9, 136-140.

Dennehy, H.G., "Naga Medicine". *Man in India*, Vol VII, (1927). Pp.196-203.

Dennis, W., "The Socialization of the Hopi Child", Language Culture and Personality : Essays in Memory of Eward Sapir, ed. L. Spir et. al. Menasha, 1941.

Desai, I.P., "The Slogan of Separate State by Tribals of South Gujarat", Research abstracts, No. 4, Indian Council of Social. Science Research, Delhi.

Desai, S.M., Horses.

Desai, S.M., "Omens for Auspicious and Inauspicious Hourses" Journal of Anthropological Society of Bombay, 1917-1921, 2 652-662.

Deuri, R.K., "Customary Laws of the Mishmis of Lohit District (Arunachal Pradesh)", Resarch Journal of the Research Department, Govt. of Arunachal Pradesh, Itanagar, 1987, 13(1-2).

Dewar, J.R., "General Description of the Naga Tribes Inhabiting the Burma Side of Patkai Range" (Census of India) Vol. III, 1931.

Devi, L. Dilly, "*Man*-Food Relationship amongt Tribes Inhabiting the Burma side of Patkai Range" Census of India), Vol. III, 1931.

Dhar, Bibhash, "Chhos Kor: The Festival of the Monpa and the Sherdukpen", *Journal of the Indian Anthropological Society*, 1982, 17(3). 265-267,

Dhar, R.M., "Socio-Economic Problems of the North Eastern Hill Region of India", in Symposeum on Soical and Economic Problems of Hilly Areas, Simla, 1974.

Dheber Commision, "Report of the Scheduled Areas and Scheduled Tribes Commissions", 1961.

Dhir, D.N., "Tribes of the North Western border of India", Read in the Seminar on Tribal Situation in India, Indian Institute of Advanced Study, Simla, 1969.

Dixon, R.B., "Social Composition of the Hindukush Tribes", 25th *Indian Science Congress*, Calcutta, 1938.

Dondrup, R., "The Migration of the Monpas of Boot area in West Kameng District", Research, Journal of the Research Deptt., Govt. of Arunachal Pradesh, Itanagar, 1987, 13 (1-2).

Doshi, S.L., "Non-Clustered Tribal Villages and Community Development", *Human Organisation*, 1969, 28(4).

Duarah, D.K., "Some Somatoscopic Characters of the Monpas of Arunachal Pradesh", Resarch, Journal of the Rcscarch Dept. Govt. of Arunachal Pradesh, Itanagar, 1987, 13 .

Duba, S.C., "Approachs to Tribal Problems in India" in Vidyarthi (ed.) Applied Anthropology, in India, Kitab Mahal, Allahabad, 1968.

Dunbar. G., "Tribes of the Brahmaputra Valley", J.R.S. London Vol. LXIII, 1958.

Dutta, P.C., "Folk Songs of the Notes of Arunachal Pradesh", Resarch, Journal of the Research Dept. Govt. of Arunachal Pradesh, Itanagar, 1987, 13 (1and2).

Dutta, S.K., "The Pascal in Tribal Folklore", *North Eastern Spectrum*, Vol. 1, July 1976, pp. 23-26.

Dutta, P.N., "Jaintia Rebellion", *Indian History Congress*, 38th Session, Utkal University, 1977, P. 410-415.

Dutta-Gupta, Joya, "Ponug Girls Association Among the Padam Abor in the Lower Abor Hills", *Bulletin of the Dept. of Anthropology*, 1960, 9(2).

Dutta-Gupta, Joya, "Ecological Balance". *Resistance*, November, 30. 1976, pp. 284.

Dutta-Gupta, Joya, "Ecological Balance", *Resistance*, December, 8. 2.

Dutta-Gupta, Joya, "Ecological Balance", *Resistance*, December, 14 287.

Dutta-Gupta, Joya, "Ecological Balance". *Resistance*, January, 4. 187.

Elkin, A.P., "Sections and Kinship in Some Desert Tribes of Austriala", *Man*, Vol. XL, pp. 21-4. 1940a.

Ehrenfels, Umar Rolf Von "Is Aboriginal Art Original?" *Man in India*, 1949, 29, 103-109.

Elliat and Dowson, "The History of India as told by its own Historians", Allahabad, Vol. III 1964, Vol.Iv, 1967.

Elmeneau, M.B., "Toda Culture through Thirty-Five Years: An Agculturation Study", Annals of Bhandarkar Oriental Research Insitute, 1938, 19 (et. II), 101-121.

Elwin, V., "A Note on the Thory of Symbolism of Dreams among the Baiga", British Journal of Medical Psychology, 1939, 26, 237-254.

Elwin, V., "Notes on the Juang", *Man in India*, 1948, 28 (1), 1-46.

Elwin, V., "Tribal Medicine in India", *Man in India*, Statesman, March 22, 1935a.

Emeneau, M.B., "Toda Garments and Embroidery", Journal of the American Oriental Society, 1937, 57, 277-289.

Emeneau, M.B., "Toda Marriage Regulations and Toboos", *American Anthropologist*, Vol. XXXIX, pp. 103-12. 1937.

Emeneau, M.B., "Kinship and Marriage Among the Corgs", *Journal of the Royal Asiatic Society of Bengal* (letters), 1938, 4. 123-147.

Emeneau, M.B., "Language and Social Forms: A Study of Toda Kinship Terms and Dual Descent" Language Culture and Personality: Essays in Memory of Edward Sapir, ed. L. Spier et. al. Menasha, 1941.

Enthoven, R.E., "Devaks in Deccan and Konkan", *Journal of the Anthropological Society of Bombay*, 1924-27, 13. 1-14.

Enthoven, R.E., "The Result of the Ethnographic Survey of Bombay", Journal of Anthropological Society of Bombay, 1921-24, 12, 113- 128.

Evan-Pritchard, E.E. "Exogamous Rules Among the Nuer", *Man* Vol. XXXV, No. 7. p. 11. 1935.

Fei, H.T., "The Problem of the Chinese Relationship System", Monumenta Serica Vol. II, pp. 125-48, 1936-7.

Ferriera, J.V., "Ethnology and History", Sociological Bulletin, 1964, 13 (1), 1-111.

Ferriera, J.V., "Katkaris and an Evaluation of Available Material", Journal of Social research, 1962 , 5 (2), 64-70.

Fisher, Captain, "Memories of the Countries on and the Eastren Frontier of Sylhet", J.A.S.B. Vol. IX.

Frake, Charles O., "The Ethnographic Study of Cognitive Behaviour, Systems", Anthropology of Human Behaviour, Washington, D.C., Anthropological Society of Washington, 1962.

Frisancho, A. R., "Human Growth and Pulmonary Funcations of a High Altitude Peruvian Quechua Population", Human Biology, 1969, 41, 365-379.

Frye, J.P., "On the Vriya and Khond Population of Orissa", *Journal of the Royal Asiatic Society* of Great Britian and Ireland, 1860, 17, 1- 38.

Furer-Haimendrof, C. Von, "Tribal Population of Hayderbad: Yesterday and Today", Census of India, 1941, 21, Hyderbad, 1945.

Furer-Haimendrof, C. Von, "Notes on the Tribal Justice among the Apei Tania", *Man in India* , 1946b, 26.

Furer-Haimendrof, C. Von, "Primitive Aboriginal Cultures in Decan", *Man in India*, 1944b, 123-128.

Furer-Haimendrof, C. Von, "Seasonal Nomadism and Economics of Chenchus of Hyderabad", Journal of Royal Asiatic Society of Bengal, 1941, s. 175-196.

Furer-Haimendrof, C. Von, "Spring Festival among the Konyak Nagas of Assam", Geographical Magazine, Vol. VII (1938), pp. 241-56.

Furer-Haimendrof, C. Von, "The Agriculture and Land Tenure among the Apei Tanis", *Man in India*, 1946a, n26 (3), 181-195.

Furer-Haimendrof, C. Von, "Aboriginal Education in Hyderabad", Indian Journal of Social Work, 1944, 5 (2), 97-186.

Furer-Haimendrof, C. Von, "The Changing Position of Tribal Populations in India", Royal Anthropological Institute News, 1977. 22, 2-8.

Furer-Haimendrof, C. Von, "The Cult of Ayak Among the Kolams of Hyderbad", Wenner Beitraur Kulturges Chichte and Linguistic, 1952, 9. 108-123.

Furer-Haimendrof, C. Von, "The Fortunes of the Primitive Tribes", Indian Journal of Social Work,1942-43, 3, 391- 406.

Furer-Haimendrof, C. Von, "The Megalithic Culture of the Naga Tribes of Assam", Research and Progress, Vol. V. No. 2 (1939). PP. 95-108

Furer-Haimendrof, C. Von, "The Morung System of the konyak Nagas, Assam", *Journal of the Royal Anthropological Institute*, Vol. LXVIII (1938). PP. 349-78.

Furer-Haimendrof, C. Von, "The Pradhans : The Boards of Raj Gond", *Eastern Anthropologist*, 1951, and (3and 4). 172-184.

Gait, E.A., "Some Notes on Jaintia History", JASB, Vol. X. 1895.

Gamini, Paul., "Anthropology and Tribal Administration", *Vanyajati*, 1957, 5 (1).

Garamble, K., "Funeral Customs of Urali", *Bulletin of the Dept. of Anthropology*. 1955b. 4 (2).

Gangte, T.S., "Search for New Identity Among the Tribals of Manipur", *Man and Life*, Vol. 10, Nos. 3and4, July- December, 1984. pp. 174-192.

Gangte, Prahab, and Pal, A., "Onge Harpoon and Spear", *Anthropos*, 1963, 58 (3-4). 557-560.

Gangte, Prahab, and Pal, A., "Geological Surver in Manipur", *Resistance*: May 0 1977, p. 2.

Gangte, Prahab, and Pal, A., "Geological Surver in Manipur", *Resistance*: May 10, 1977, p. 2.

Gangte, Prahab, and Pal, A., "Geological Surver in Manipur", *Resistance*: May 17, 1977, p. 2.

Ghate, B.G., Study of the Population Movement in India", Indian Journal of Economics, January, 1939.

Ghosh, A.K., "Selection Intensity in the kota of Nilgiri Hills", Madras, Social Biology, 1970, 17, 224-225.

Ghosh, A., R.L. Kirk, S, Joshi and H. Bhatia, "Population Genetic Study of the Kota in the Nilgiri HillsSouth India", *Human Heredity*, 1977, 27, 225-241.

Ghurye, G.S., A Note of the Cross Cousin Marrige and Daul Organisation in Kathiawar", Journal of the University of Bombay, 1936-3, 5 (1), 88-90.

Ghurye, G.S., "Dual Organisation in India", Journal of Royal Anthropological Institute, 1923, 53, 679-691.

Gibbs, E.T., "Bhils in the Dargs", Indian Antiguary, 1876. 5. 83.

Gibson, A., "Notes on the Bhils of North of the Nerbada", ournal of the Bombay Branch of Royal Asiatic Society, 1867-70, 9.1-11.

Gimson, C., "Some Notes on the Maring Nagas of Manipur", *Man in India*, 6; 277-94. 1920.

Gnanamble, K., "The Kanikkars of Tranvancore, Their Religious and Magical Practices", *Bulletin of the Dept. of Anthropology*. 1954, 3 (2),

Gnanamble, K., "The Magical Rites of Uralis (Agriculture, Puberty, Pregnancy and Curing of Diseases)", *Bulletin of the Dept. of Anthropology*, 195a, 4 (2).

Godden, G.M., "Naga and Other Frontier Tribes of North East India", *Journal of the Royal Anthropological Institute*, Vol. XXVI, pp. 161-201, 1895.

Godden, G.M., "Naga and other Frontier Tribes of North-East India, Contd.", *Journal of the Royal Anthropological Institute*, Vol. XXVI, pp. 22-51. 1897.

Godwin-Austen H.H., "Naga Movements", Indian Antiguary, Vol. II, (1973), p. 214.

Godwin-Austen H.H., "On the Rude Stone Movements of Certain Naga Tribes, with some remarks on their Customs", *Journal of the Anthropological Institute*, Vol. IV (1874), pp. 144-7.

Godwin-Austen H.H., "Report on the Survey Operations in the Naga Hills and Manipur During the Firld Season 1872-73", General Report on the Topographical Surveys of India for the Season. 1872-73, App. 74-87.

Godwin Austin, H.S., "Notes on the Wild Tribes Inhabitating the so called Naga Hills on Over N.E. Frontier of India", *J.A.T. London*, Vol. XI, 1882.

Gohain, B.C., "Agricultural Organisation Among the Abor", *Bulletin of the Deptt. Of Anthropology*, 1954. 3 (2).

Gohain, Krishna, M.S., "The Cute of Musher Goddess", in Balarathnam (ed.) Anthropology on the Mareh, Social Science Asociation. Madras, 1963, 334-351.

Goldenwieiser, A.A. "Remarks on the Social Organization of the Crow Indians", *American Anthropologist*, Vol. XVm pp. 281-94, 1913.

Goswami B.B., "Kinship System of the Lushai", Bulletin of the Department of Anthropology, 1960, 3 (2).

Goswami B.B., "Tribe to Peasant not Caste: Some Comments on Mizo Situation", *The Eastren Anthropologist*, 1978, 31 (9).

Goswami M.G., "The Garo of Meghalaya and their Neighbour", in The Tribal Peopal of India, New Delhi, 1973.

Goswami, M.G. and Ch. Buddhi Singh, "Co-operatives of the Fisherman of Thanga Village in Manipur", *Man in India*, LIII, 1973. 1. 1-6.

Goswami, P., "NagaTales", *Eastern Anthropologist*, Vol. VIII, 1954-5, pp. 73-78.

Gough, Kathleen, "Cult of the Dead Among the Nayars", in Milton Singer (ed.) Traditional American Folklore Society, Philadelphia, 1959, 240-271.

Govt. of Manipur, Directorate Of Economics and Statistics,"Economic Review" (Annaul Series): 1978-86.

Govt. of Manipur, Planning and Development Department., "District Council Manual", Vol. I, Imphal, 1972.

Government of Manipur, "Hand Book of Manipur Hill Village Authority", Imphal.

Graham Hower, "Cycle-Migration of the Zemi Nagas", *Man in India*, Vol. 26. 1976, pp. 50-

Grange, G.L. "Extracts From the Journey of an expedition to the Naga Hills on the Assam Frontier", JASB – 1840.

Grant, F.T., "Extracts from a Journal kept During a tour of Inspection on the Manipur frontier along the Course of the Ningthee River, Janural 1832", *Journal of the Asiatic Society of Bengal*, 3; 124-34, 1834.

Grierson, W.V., "The Aboriginal in the Future India", Journal of Royal Anthropological Institute of Great Britian and Ireland, 1944, 74, 34-41.

Grierson C., "Some Notes on the Maring Nagas of Manipur", *Man in India*, Vol. 1903, pp. 277-94.

Growse, F.S., "The Art of 'Tar-Kashi or Wire-Inlay as Practised by Carbenters of Manipur in the North- West provinces", Journal Of Indiar Art and Industry, 1888, 2 (22) 51-56.

Guha, B. S., "Indian Aborigines and who they are, The Adivasis, The Publication Division, Ministry of Information and Broadcasting, Govt. of India, 1958, 31.

Guha, Amalendu, "A Historiographical Perspective for North-East India:, *Man in India*, Vol. 622. 1982, p. 221.

Guha, B.S. and Basu, C.P., "A Report on the Human Relics Recovered by the naga Hills (Burma) Expedition for the abolition of Human Sacrifice during 1926-7" Anthropological Bulletin from the Zoological Survey of India (Cal. 1931).

Guha, B.S., "Report of a Suurvey of the Inhabitants of Andaman and Nicobar Islands during 1948-49", Bulletiin of the Dept. of Anthropology, 1952, 1-7.

Guha, B.S., "The Aboriginal Races in India", *Science and Culture*, 1938-39, 4 (12), 677-683.

Guha, Kamalesh, "Tribal Handicrafts in India", *Vanyajati*. 1960, 8. 117-123.

Guha, P.K., "Shompen: A Primitive Tribe in Transition" (Great Nicobar Island). *Man in India*, 1988, 68 (4), 465-469.

Gulati, P.V., "Mortality Rate and Causes of Deaths Among the Children Below Five Years A field Study in a Semi Urban Area of Delhi", Indian Joutnal of Pediatries, April, 1967.

Gunthorpe, E.J., "Notes on the Bhonde Koomars", *Journal of the Anthropological Society of Bombay*, 1886-89, 1. 409-414.

Gupta, Kalyan Kumar Das, "The Kulutas: An Early Indian Tribe", *Journal of Indian History* Vol. LV. April, August, 1977, Part. land II, pp. 11-23.

Gupta, Pabitra, Biman Kumar Dasgupta, Arbinda Basu and Bikash Rarchaudhuri, "The Chote (Phurum) of Manipur some Sociological and Demographic Observations" *Man in India*, Vol. 55, 1975, p. 239.

Hajong, Abani Kumar, The Hajongs", *North Eastern Spectrum,* Vol. II, July, 1977, NO. 1, pp. 16-18.

Hazirika, Munindra P., "Cultural Development in Arunachal Pradesh", *Spectrum,* Vol. V. July, 1976. No. 1 pp. 39-40.

Hebderg, E., "The Celebration of Devali by the Newa Bhils", *Journal of the Anthropological Society of Bombay,* 1924-28, 13 854-892.

Hendley, T.H., "An Account of Maiwar Bhils", *Journal of Asiatic Society of Bengal,* 1875, 44, 347-388.

Hendley, T.H., "Hill Peoples Regulation", *Resistance,* Nov. 8, 1977, pp.6-7., Nov. 15, 1977, pp. 6-7., Nov. 22, 1977 pp. 7, 7 and 8.

Hippolytus, "The Relations Between Religion and Morality Among the Bhils", *Primitive Man,* 1931, 1931 4. 49-53.

Hocart, A.M.m "The Indo-European Kinship System", *Ceylon Journal of Science* (Section-G) Vol. I, art-4, 49-53.

Hodgson, B.H., "The Aborigines of the Eastern Frontier" *Journal of the Royal Asiatic Society of Bengal* 1948, 18. (Part-II) 967-975.

Hodson, T.C., "Notes on the Marriage of Cousins in India", *Man in India,* Vol. V. pp. 163-75. 1925.

Hodson, T.C., "The Native Tribes of Manipur", *Journal of the Anthropological Institute,* Vol. IV, 1901, pp. 300-309.

Hodson, T.C., "Nagas", *Encyclopadia of Religion and Ethics,* Vol. IX, 1916, pp. 123-5.

Hodson, T.C., "Some Naga Coustoms and Superstitions", *Folk-lore* Vol. XXI (1910), pp. 296-312.

Hodson, T.C., "Manipur and Its Tribes", *Journal of the Royal Society of Arts* 53: 545., 1905.

Horam, M., "The Manipur Society. A Brief Sociological Study", *North-Eastern Spectrum,* Pan Bazar, Gauhati, Vol. II No. 7-8. Jan-Feb. 1978.

Horam, M., "Social Change in Nagaland", *Man in India,* Vol. 55. 1975, p. 149.

Horne, C., "Notes on Himalayan Villages in Kumaon, Garhwal and on the Satlej", *Indian Antiquary,* Education Society Press, Bombay, 1876, pp. 161-167.

Hughes, H. Stuart, "The Historian and the Social Scientist", *American Histcrical Review,* 1960, 66: 20-46.

Hussain, I.Z. "Demographic Challeage to Economic Development in Asia", in *Indian Population Bulletin,* Office of the Registrar General, New Delhi, 1966.

Hussain, S.K.M., "Medicine Among the Gonds, Kolams and Chenchus", *Man in India,* 1950, 30, pp. 23-31.

Hussain, S.K.M. "Koyas", *Man in India,* 1951, 31 (1), 33-39.

Hutton, J.H., "Leopard Man in the Naga Hills", *Journal of the Royal Anthropological Institute,* Vol. L. (1920), pp. 41-51.

Hutton, J.H., "Thadou Kuki Terms of Relationship", *Man in India* Vol.2. 1922, p. 108.

Hutton, J.H., "The Connection of Different Nagas and other Tribes in Assam", *Census of India,* 1921, 1923, 3, pp. XXI-XXVI.

Hutton, J.H., "The Meaning and Method of the Creation of Monoliths by the Naga Tribes", *Journal of the Royal Anthropological Insititute,* Vol. LXI (1922), pp, 242-9.

Hutton, J.H., "Head Hunting", *Encyclopadia Britannica,* 14th ed. Vol. XVI. 1929, p. 59.

Hutton, J.H., "A Note on the Method of Skull Oranmentation Practised Among the Konyak Nagas of Assam", *Man* Vol. XXIX, No. 158 (1929).

Hutton, J.H., "Mokola: A chang Naga Folk-Tale Regarding, the Relation Between a Man and His Sister's Son", *Man in India* Vol. II (1922), pp. 100-103.

Hutton, J.H., "Two Celts from the Naga Hills", *Man in India,* Vol. 22 1922. pp. 104

Hutton, J.H., "The Mixed Culture of the Naga Tribes", *Journal of the Royal Anthropological Institute,* Vol. LXVI (1945), pp. 1-7.

Hutton, J.H., "The Significance of Head-Hunting in Assam", *Journal of the Anthropological Institute Royal*, Vol. LVIII (1928), pp. 399-408.

Hutton, J.H., "A Konyak Naga Snare", *Man*, Vol. XXII, No. 103. (1922).

Hutton, J.H., Angami Naga Dye Processes", *Man* , Vol. XXIII, No. 22. (1923).

Hutton, J.H., "The Disposal of the Dead at Wakching", *Man,* Vol XXVII, No. 44 (1927).

Hutton, J.H., "Divided and Decorated Heads as Trophies", *Man* Vol. XXII, No. 67. (1922).,

Hutton, J.H., "Clan Monopoly of Personal Names", *Man*, Vol. XXXIX, No. 61 (1939).

Hutton, J.H., "Ethnographic Notes by Various Hands" *Census of India,* 1931, 1. (Part-IIIB) P. 243.

Hutton, J.H., "Folk-Tales of the Angami Nagas with Notes", *Folk-lore*, Vol. XXV, No. 4 (1914), pp. 476-498). 8 Vol. XXVI, No. 1 (1915), pp.82-8.

Hutton, J.H., "Naga Chank Ornaments of S. Indian Affinities", *Man,* Vol. XXVI, No. 145 (1926).

Hutton, J.H., "Note on a Type of Snare from the Phom Country", *Man* Vol. XXII, No. 63 (1922).

Hutton, J.H., "Occurrence of Blow-Gun in Assam", *Man*, Vol. XXIV No. 29 (1924).

Hutton, J.H., "A Negrito Substratum in the Population of the Assam", *Man in India*, Vol. VII, 1927), pp. 257-262.

Hutton, J.H., "Diaries of two Tours in the Unasministered Area East of the Naga Hills", *Memories of the Asiatic Society of Bengal*, Vol. XI (1929).

Hutton, J.H., "Assam and the Pacific", *Man in India,* !924, 4(1), pp. 1-13.

Iyer, L.A. Krishna, "Marriage Customs Among the Muthuvans of Travancore", *Man in India,* 1924, 4.

Iyer, L.A. Krishna, "Matriarchy in Kerala", *Man in India*, 1944, 24 (1).

Iyer, L.A. Krishna, "Some Aspects of the Material Culture of the Primitive Tribes of South India", *Man in India,* 1949, 29. pp. 76-83.

Iyer, L.A. Krishna, "Taboo Among the Primitive Tribes of Travancore", *Quatterly Journal of the Mythic Society,* 1934-35, 25. pp. 95-102.

Iyer, L.A. Krishna, "The Religion of the Primitive Tribes of Travancore", *Journal of Mythic Society,* Bangalore, 1934, 24 (3).

Iyer, L.A. Krishna, "Matriarchy in Kerala", *Journal of Mythic Society of Bangalore* 1960-61, 51.

Jahagirdar, M.P. "The Status and Role of Women in a Tribal Community", *Man in India,* 1988, 68(4), 424-430.

Jain, P.K., "Marriage Age Patterns in India", *Artha Vijanana* XI (4), 1959.

Jain, S.P., "Indian Fertitity and Knowledge and Gaps", *Journal of Fmilu Welfare*. X (4), 1964.

Jaswal, I.J.S., "Search for early man in North-East India", *Man in India,* Vol. 56, 1976. p. 276.

Jay, Edward., "A comparision of Tribal and Peasant Villages in India", *Journal of the Indian Anthropological Society,* 1974, 9 (1), 39-69.

Jay, Edward., "*The Anthropologists* and Tribal welfare: Hill Marias – A Case Study", in Vidyarthi (ed.) *Anthropology and Tribal welfare in India,* 1968.

Jay, Edward, J., "Structural Obstacles to Tribal Accuturation : The Case of Regiona Ceremonial Integration in Baster", *Eastern Anthropologist,* 1965, 18(3), 159-163.

Jayakar, Pupul, "Some Terracota Figurines from Tribal Gujarat", *Marg,* 1953, 7 (1) 23-32.

Jenkins, F., "Report No. 309 of 1853 on Relations with Hill Tribes on the Assam Frontier", Mills, *Report on the province of Assam,* 1854, App. M, pp. 117-66.

Jerol, S., "The History and Culture of the Anals", Presented in *Seminar on the History of Manipur,* 1975, Imphal: Centre for Post Graduate Studies in History, Jawaharlal Nehru University.

Jha, J.C., "The Tribal Society of Kolhan (Singhbhum) at the advent of British rule in 1837-8" *Indian History Congress,* 38th Session, Utkal University, 1977, pp. 500-510.

Joginder Kumar, "Human Fertility – A Complex Process", Journal of Social Sciences, (Agra), Dec. 1965.

Lahiri, R., "Settlement Types in Ajay-Barkar Basin", *Culcutta Geographical Review,* 1950, 12 (4).

Kabui, Gangmumei, " Social and Religious Reform Movement in Manipur in the 19th and 20th Centuries", *Bulletin of the Division of History,* Imphal, Centre of Post Graduate Studies J.N.U., 1974, 53-75.

Kabui, Gangmumei, "Our Indigenous People the Anal", *Resistance*: September 7, 1976, pp. 3-4., September 14, p.3, September 21, 1976 pp. 3-4, September 28, 1976 pp. 3-4.

Kabui, Gangmumei, "Point of View – The Problem of Identity among the Anal Tribe", *Resistance,* Jan. 4 1977, pp. 3-4.

Kabui, Gangmumei, " Our Indigenous Peoples – The Tarao – A Forgotten Tribe of Manipur", *Resistance* November, 2, 1976, pp. 3-4., November, 9, 1976, p. 3.

Kabui, Gangmumei, "Point in View – Zeliangrong Movement, 1927-1977: A brief History", *Resistance,* January, 10, 1978, pp. 3-4., January, 17, 1978 pp. 3-4., January 24, 1978, pp. 3-4.

Kabui, Gangmumei, "Political Development in the Hill Areas of Manipur : Third Summer School in the Sociology of India, Kohima, 1970.

Kabui, Gangmumei, "*The Land System of the Rongmei Tribe of* Manipur, (Unpublished).

Kalia, S.L., "Sanskritisation and Tribalisation", *Bulletin of the Tribal Research Institute,* Chindwara, April, 1959, 33-43.

Kamkhenthang, H., "Our Indigenous Peoples – The Paite – In Present Perspective", *Resistance* January, 25. 1977, p.3. February, 1. 1977 pp. 3-4.

Kamkhenthang, H., n.d., "The Moyon-Monsang Folk Tales", *Directorate for Welfare of Tribal and Backward Classes.* Govt. of Manipur, Imphal.

Kamson, Meijingung, " The Cunstoms and Traditions of the Kabuis", *Manipur State Kala Academy. Quarterly Journal*, 1 and 4, 1-21.

Kapoor, D., "People of Kinnaur – An Eassay in the Problem of Tribes", (Presented in the Seminar on Situation in India), *Indian Institute of Advance Study, Simla,* 1969.

Kar, Biman, "Tripura in the Limelight", *North Eastern Spectrum,* Vol. II. March – July, 1978, No. 9-11, pp. 25-28.

Kar, R.K., "A Migrant Tribe in a Tea Plantation in India : Economic Profile", *Anthropos,* 1976, 74 (5 and 6) , 770-84.

Kar, R.K., "Unity in Diversity : A Note on the Process of Adaptation of a Tribe in a Tea Industry", *Bulletin of the Dept. of Anthropology,* D.U., 1975, 4. 11-15.

Kar, L.N., "Pattern of Tribal Education: A Psychological Approach", *Journal of the University of Gauhati,* 1957, 8. 59-72.

Kar, L.N., "The Role of Teachers in a Tribal Community", *Journal of the University of Gauhati,* 1962, 13 (1), 57-63.

Karmarkar, A.D., "Some Socio-Economic and Demographic Features of Sterlised Females in Belgaum District during 1968-69", *Journal of Institute of Economic Research,* July, 1970.

Karup, R.S. and George N.U., "Variations in Fertility Between Two Generation", Demographic Research Centre, Tribandrum, *Journal of Family Welfare,* 15(4).

Karup, .S.S., "Need for increased attention to Family Planning in the Context of the Economic Development in Kerala State", *Participant Journal,* May, 1968.

Karve, Irawati, "Kinship Terminology and Kinship Uses of the Maratha Country", "*Bulletin of the Deccan College Research Insititute,* Ponna, 1940-41. 2-4.

Karve, Irawati, "Bhils of Western Khandesh", *Journal of Anthropological Soceity of Bombay,* 1958.

Karve, Irawati, "Social Education of Scheduled Tribes" *Vanyajati,* 1957, 5 (4), 164-169.

Karve, Irawati, "The Tribals of Maharastra, In Beharilal Abbi and Satish Sabarwal (eds.)" *Urgent Research in Social Anthropology in India,* Institute of Advance Study, Simla, 1959.

Karth, G. Rajani and Chandra, K. Suman, "Education of Tribals – The Role Tribal Political Orgainstation", *Man in India* 1988, 68 (4), 459-464.

Kauffman, H.F. "Die Spiele der Thadou – Kuki in Assam", *Zeitschrift fur Ethnologic,* 1941, 73.

Kauffman, H.F., "The Thread-Square Symbol of the Nagas of Assam", *Journal of the Royal Anthropological Insitute,* Vol. LXXII, (1943) pp. 101.

Kuffmann, Walter, "The Musical Instruments of the Hill Maria and Bastar Muria Gond Tribes", *Ethno-Musicology,* 1961, 5(1), 1-9.

Kaul, S.K., "Existing Facilities, Coverage, Wastage, Stagnation and Utilisation of Financial Assistance in respect of Tribal Education", *In Tribal Education in India,* N.C.E.R.T., Delhi, 1967.

Kazi, Tubaki, "Physical Anthropological Study on the Tribals in Bihar : Oraon, Munda, Santal and Paharia including the Caste Peoples", *Proceeding of the Indian Secience Congress,* 1968, Part-3, 55th Session, Varanasi-30.

Khan, G.A., "The Chenchus", in J.P. Mills and Others (eds)., *Essays in Anthropology Presented to Rai Bahadur,* S.C. Roy, Maxwell and Co. Lucknow, 1942, 261-264.

Khan, M.E., "A Report on Factors Affecting Spacing of Births", *Demographic Research Centre,* Dept. of Statistics Mimeographe Service No. 18, Patna University, Patna, 1972.

Khanapurkar, D.P., "Gupan, An Adivasi Tribe of South Gujarat: Its Sub-Divisions and Their Formation", *Journal of the University of Bombay,* 1946-47, 15 (Part-I), 51-52.

Kharend, T.P. (Dy. Secy, N.E.C.), "Documentation of the Various Facets of Tribal Society in North Eastern Region", *Journal of*

North Eastern Council, May-June, 1985, Vol.VII, No. 5 and 6, pp. 28-30.

Kipgen, Khaikhotinthang, "Our Indigenous Peoples – The Moyons – Soceity and Culture", *Resistance* October. 19, 1975. p. 3., October. 26, 1976. p. 3.

Kipgen, Khaikhotinthang, "Our Indigenous Peoples – The Thadous", *Resistance*, October 5, 1976, p.3.

King, Rev. C.D., "Naga Mode of Harvesting, Resieged in the Nage Hills and Other Articles", *Baptist Missionary Magazine*, Vol. LX (1879), pp. 15-16, 32-6, 69-71, 100-2, 151-2 and 419-20.

Kirk, R.L., "A Genetical Study of the Oraons of the Chota Nagpur Plateau (Bihar)", *American Journal of Physical Anthropology, 1962,* 20, 375-385.

Kitson, E.R., Mount, G. "A Study of the Naga Skull", *Biometrika* Vol. XXV, 1933, pp.-20.

Kiulin, J.E., "Correlater of Family Planning in Eight Indian Villages", *Research Report – 18th Project on the Diffusion of Innovation in Rural Society*, National Institute of Community Development, Hyderabad, 1968.

Khinman, D.S., "Observations on Economic Correlates of Rural Fertility in India", *Population Review*, Dec. 1970.

Koli, B.R. and Vohra, "Fertility Control in India", *Camily Planning News,* 5(1) and 5(2), 1964.

Kondel, J., "Infant Mortality and Fertility in Three Bavarina Villages: An Analysis of Family Histories from the 19th Century", *Population Studies,* XXII (3), 1968.

Koshi, Elizabeth, P., "Study of the Menstrual Pattern of School Girls in an Urban Area", *Indian Journal of Medical Research* 1st November. 1970.

Koppers, W., "India and the Dual Organisation", *Acta Tropica,* 1944, 1. 72-92, 97-119.

Krishnamoorthy, K., "Fertility and Mortility Levels in two Community Development Blocks", *Bulletin of Gandhigram Institute of Rural Health and Family Planning,* 6(1).

Krishnan, B.K., "Diet Survey in the Nilgiris and Travbancore", *Indian Journal of Medical Research,* 1939.

Krishna Swami, V.D., Prehistoric Bastar" PISC (40th Session), Lucknow, 1953.

Kshetri, Rajendra, "Tribal Social System of Manipur: Some Aspects", in Gangmumei Kabui (ed.) *Tribal Profile of Manipur,* Centre for Tribal Studies, M.U. 1990, pp.48-

Kshetri, Agenda, "The Paite: A Transborder Tribe of India and Burma, Book Review in *Quarterly Journal,* MSKA, Imphal September. 1989, pp. 84-86.

Kumar, N. and D.P. Mukherjee, "Genetic Distances Among the Ho Tribe of other Group of Central India", *American Journal of Physical Anthropology,* 1975, 42, 489-94.

Kumar, Dutta, Dilip, "From Pre-History to History : A schematic View of Culture in the Tribal World of North East India", *Bulletin of the Deptt. Of Anthropology,* Dibrugarh University, 1975, 4, 16-40.

Kumar, N., "Taste, Middle-Phalngral Hair and Occipital Hair Whols Among Nokte Naga", *Bulletin of the Deptt. of Anthropology* Vol. IV No. 2 Calcutta, 1954.

Kumar, N. and D.B. Sastry, "A Genetic Survey Among the Riang A Mongloid Tribe of Tripura", *Morphological Anthropology,* 1961, 51 346-355.

Lakshmaiah, T. and Yadappanvar, Aravind, " A study of Educational Facilities for Tribal Students-Problems and Impact in Paderu Samithi in Andhra Pradesh", *Man in India,* 1988, 68(4), 380-400.

Lal, A., "Infant Mortality, Some Socio-Economic and Biological Determinants. *Indian Journal of Child Health,* No. 11, 1962.

Lal Dena, "Coloialism and Christian Mission in Manipur A Study", *Resistance*, October 12, 1976.

Lal Dena, """Hmar People Boycott Movement 1, II, and III. *Resistance* July, 13, 1976, p.3. July 20, 1976 p. 3. July 27, 1976, p.3.

Lal Dena, "Point of View-Political Development in the Hills : A Rapid Survey in Colonial Perspective", *Resistance,* April 26, 1977, pp. 3-4.

Lal Manohar, "Elite and Development in Munda Society", *Man and Life,* 1984, 10(3and4), 147-158.

Lambert, E.T.D., "Human Sacrifices in Assam", *Journal of the Assam Research Society,* Vol. VI. (1938-9), pp. 65-7.

Leuwa, K.K., "Social Education – The Sheet of Anchor of Tribal Welfare", *Report of the Fourth Conference for Tribes and Tribal Areas,* New Delhi, 1967, 73-74.

Lian, Za OO, "Our Indigenous Peoples The Chin", *Resistance,* November 28, 1978, pp. 3-4. December 5, 1978, pp. 3-4.

Lightfoot, G.S., "Ringing A Tiger in the Naga Hills", *Assam Review,* (May, 1929).

Livingstone, F.B., "A Further Analysis of Purum Society", *American Anthropologist,* 1959, 61.

Loeb, E.M., "Patrilineal and Matrilineal Organistion in Sumatra : The Batak and the Minangkabau", *American Anthropologist,* Vol. XXXV, pp. 16-50. 1933.

Lowie, Robbert H., *"Oral Tradition and History"* PP. 202-210 in Robert H. Lowie, Selected Papers in *Anthropology* edited by Cora Dubois, Burkeley University of California Press, 1960.

Madan, T.N., "Education of Tribal India", *Eastern Anthropologist,* 1952, 5(4) 179-182.

Mahalingam, T.V., "The Nagas in Indian History and Culture *Journal of Indian History,* Trivandrum, April, 1965.

Mahanta, J. and K.C. Panda, "Mantal Health, Achievement, Motivation and Jhang acculturation", *Journal of the Indian Anthropological Society,* 1982, 17 (2), 129-142.

Mahanta, K.C., "Socio-Economic Changes in an immigrant Sema Village in Assam", *Bulletin of the Department of Anthropology,* Dibrugarh University, 1978-79, 7 and 8,132-141.

Mahapatra, L.K., "Curricular Methods and Text-Books in Tribal Education", *Tribal Education in India* N.C.E.R.T., New Delhi, 1967, 109-120.

Mahapatra, L.K., "Ditermining Social Types on the Tribe Peasant Continuum, *Journal of Indian Anthropological Society,* 1974, 9(1), 71-83.

Mahapatra, L.K., "Education Old and New', *Orissa Tribes Research Journal,* (Inaugural Number), 1955, 23-33.

Mahapatra, L.K., "Food Quest Among the Pauri Bhuiyan' *Eastern Anthropologist,* 1956, 9(1), 48-52.

Mahapatra, L.K., "From Shifting Cultivation to Agriculturist-The Pauri Bhuiyan in Transition', *Archiv*, 1965-66, 10 and 11 (2), 31-48.

Mahapatra, L.K., "The Chenenga Kullis of Bonai, Orissa: Their Changing Economy', *Baessler-Archiv,* Neue Folge Band XI, 347-359 (n.d)

Mahapatra, L.K., "The Dahala and Miji Society: A Preliminary Ecological Analysis', *Sociologus,* 1962, 12 (2), 158-167.

Mahapatra, U.D., "Study of Fertility in a Tribe of North East India (Khasi) "*Journal of Social Research,* 1970, 30, 74-82.

Mahato, S. (Ranchi), "Chotanagpur Mission During the Indian Rebellion (1875-58)", *Indian History Congress*, 31st Session, Vanarasi Patna, 1970, p. 375-381.

Majumdar, D.N., "Tribal Culture and Accurturation", *Man in India,* 1939, 19, 99-170.

Majumdar, D.N., "A Study of Tribe Caste Continuum and The Process of Sanskritization Among the Bodo Speaking Tribes of Garo Hills", *In Tribal Situation in India,* J.S. Singh (ed.), Indian Institute of Advanced Study, Simla , 1972.

Majumdar, D.N., " A Few remarks on the Sema Naga Kinship Terms", *Man in India,* Vol. IV (1924), pp. 193-208.

Majumdar, D.N., "A Study of Sanskritisation Among the Bodo speaking trubes of Garo Hills" Read in Seminar on *Tribal Situation in India,* Indian Institute of Advanced Study, Simla, 1969.

Majumdar, D.N., "The Ao Nagas", *Man in India*, Vol. 4, 1924, P.41.

Majumdar, M.P.N., "The Bhils of Gujarat "*Modern Review* 1927, 41, 206-302.

Majumdar, Murari and Dasgupta, Ajit, "Marriage trends and their Demographic Implication", *Sangkhya Series,* B. 312, (3 and 4), 1969.

Majumdar, Nilima, "Abor House Type "*Indian Science Congress Association,* Poona (Part-III), 1950.

Man, B.S., "Family Planning among the Tribals", *Family Planning News,* 1968, 9(3), 15-17.

Man, Edward Horace, "Discriptive Catalogue of Objects used by the Natives of the Nicober Islands", *Indian Antiquary,* 1895.

Man, E.H., "The Aboriginal Inhabitants of the Andaman Islands", *Journal of the Anthropological Institute,* 1883, 12, 379-383.

Mani, S.B., "Bows and Arrows in Tribal India", *Vanvajati,* 1964, 12 (1), 40-45.

Manish Rajan Chakravarti and Deba Prasad Mukherji, "Dermatoglyphic Study on the Tribes and Castes of Nagaland and Manipur State", *Bulletin of the Anthropological Survey* of India, 21.

Mankad, B.L., "Rabaris of Kathiawar", *Journal of the University of Bombay,* 1938-39, 7 (pt.4), 31-71.

Man, K. (Mrs.), "Status of Bhil and Khasi Women : A Comparative study", *Journal of North-Eastern Council,* May-June, 1986, Vol. VII, Nos. 5 and 6, pp. 42-46.

Man, R.S., "Position of Women in Tribal Rajasthan" Tribal Women in India, *Indian Anthropological Society,* 1978.

Masters, J.W., "Extract from a Memoir of Some of the Natural Production of the Angami Naga Hills and other Parts of Upper Assam", *Journal of the Asiatic of Bengal,* Vol. XVII, pt. 1, 1848, pp. 57-59.

Mandal, B.B., "Are Tribal Cultivator to be called Peasants "*Man in India,* 1975.

Mandelbann, D.G., "Technology Credit and Culture in a Nilgiri Village", in M.N. Srinivas (ed.) *India's Villages*, Asia Publishing House Bombay, 1955.

Mandelbanm, D.G., "The World and the World View of the Kota", in Merrior (ed.), *Village India,* Chicago University Press, Chicago, 1935.

Mathur, K.S., "Socio-Economic Survey of Primitive Tribes of Madhya Pradesh", National Council of Applied Economic Research, Delhi, 1963.

Mathur, J.S., "Tribal Development in Administration in India", in Vidyarthi (ed.) *Applied Anthropology in India,* Kitab Mahal Allahabad, 1968.

Mathur, K.S., "Tribe in India: A Problem of Idetigication and Integration', *The Tribal Situation in India* (ed.) K.S. Singh, semdan, *Indian Institute of Advanced Study*, 1972.

Mc. Connal, U., "Social Organisation of the Tribes of Cape York Peninsula, North Queensland' *Oceania* Vol,. X. pp. 56-72, 434-55, 1940.

Medhi, Gopal Chandra, "Traditional Administration of the Karbis, *North Eastern Spectrum,* Vol. II, July, 1977. No. 1, pp. 26-28.

Medhi, B.K., " Beliefs, rituals and ceremonies connected with Principal events of the Life of the Pati Rabhas of Assam', *Bulletin of the Department of Anthropology,* Dibrugarh University, 1980, 9. 0-53.

Mehra, D.S. and Kundra J.D., "A Study of the Scheduled Castes and the Scheduled Tribes working forces in India' *AICC Economic Review,* 1966, 18(8), 31-36, and 39 and 41.

Mehta, B.H., "A Summary of the Survey of the Economic Life of an Aboriginal Tribe of Gujarat', *Journal of University of Bombay,* 1934, 2, 311-364.

Medhi, Gopal Chandra, "The Route of Karbi Migration to Assam', *North Eastern Specturm,* Vol. I, September-October 1976, No. 3 and 4, pp. 9-13.

Meinam, Binota Devi, " *A Study of Fertility and Mortality in Relation to Socio-Economic Development of Manipur – a Case Study of Imphal"* (Unpub. Ph.D. Thesis) Manipur University Canchipur, Imphal., 1989.

Meinam, Binota Devi, "Tribal Economy and Demographic Trends in Manipur" *Tribal Profile of Manipur,* (ed.) By Gangmumei Kabui, Centre for Tribal Studies, M.U. Canchipur, 1990.

Melevani, Mona, "The Changing Scene in Shillong" *North Eastern Spectrum*, Vol. I, November 1976, No.5, pp. 49-50.

Mills, J.P., "Certain Aspects of Naga Culture", *Journal of the Royal Anthropological Institute,* Vol. LVI, 1926, pp. 27-35.

Mills, J.P., "A Lhota Naga-Apotia Death", *Journal of the Indian Anthropological Institute,* Vol. I 1938, pp. 23-27.

Mills, J.P., "Folk-stories in Lhota Naga", *Journal of the Royal Asiatic Soceity of Bengal,* Vol. XXII, (N.S. 1926), pp. 235-318.

Mills, J.P., "Mammals of the Naga Hills", *Journal of the Bombat Natural History Society*, Vol. XXIX, 1923.

Mills, J.P., "The Ethics of Head Hunting", *Discoveryl, June, 1935.*

Mills, J.P., "The effects of Ritual upon Industries and Arts in the Naga Hills', No. 144, 1935.

Mills, J.P., "The Effects on the Naga Tribes of Assam of Their Contact with Western Civilisations', *Proceeding of 5th Pacific Science Congress* Vol. IV, (Toronto, 1934) pp2871-82.

Mills, J.P., "The Custom of Temporary Marriage Among the Eastern Angami Nagas", *Man,* No. 156, 1937.

Mills, J.P., "The Naga Head Hunters of Assam" *Royal Central Asian Journal,* Vol. XXII (1935) pp. 418-24.

Mills, J.P., "Some Recent Contact Problems in the Khasi Hills", J.P. MILLS (ed.) *Essay in Anthropological* Presented to S.C.Roy, Maxwell and Co. Lucknow, 1948.

Mills, J.P., "The Rengma Nagas - A split Tribe", *Man* Vol. XXXV (1935). Pp. 419-51.

Mills, J.P., "The Sacred Chiefs of Assam", *Man in India,* Vol. XXVIII (1948), pp. 149-51.

Mishra, Gitanjali, "Impact of Development Schemes: A Hill Juang Village of Orissa", *Journal of the* Indian Anthropologist, 1983, 17(2), 52(2).

Mishra, Rajlakshmi, "Inter-Tribal Relations in Erumadu", *The Eastern Anthropologist,* 1972, 52(2).

Misra, A., "Note of Tour of the Andaman and Nicobar Islands". *Bulletin of the Anthropological Survey of India,* 1962, 11(1). 1-11.

Mitra, P.N., "Blood Groups of the Angami Naga and the Lushai Tribes", *Indian Journal of Medical Research,* Vol. XXIII (1936). Pp. 685-686.

Mitra, K.P. "The Ao Nagas", *Man in India*, Vol. IV (1924), pp. 41-82.

Mitra, S.C., "The Magical Conflict in Santali Bengali and Ao Naga Folk-Lore", *Man in India,* Vol. 9, 1929. p. 173.

Mitra, S.C., "On a Meithei Apologue and its Bengali Variant", *Man in India,* 1925. 5.

Modi, J.J., "The Aghukheh of the Sema Nagas of the Assam Hills and the Chah of the Kabuis", *Journal of the Anthropological Society of Bombay,* Vol. XII (1922), pp. 609-16, About the use of pits as trapsin battle.

Monoharan, S., "Linguistic effect of culture contact: Present Andmanese Linguistic situation", *Journal of the India Anthropological Society,* 1982, 17(3), 223-228.

Mookherji, Ajit, "Adivasi Arts and Crafts", *Macrh in India,* 1961, 13 (2), 7.

Mookerji, R.K., "The Nokrom System of the Garos of Assom" *Man*, Vol. XXXIX, Nos. 167, p. 168, 1939.

Morgan, L.H., "Systems of Consanguinity and Affinity of the Anwan Family", South Asian Contributions of Knowledge, Vol. XVII, No. 218, Washington, 1971.

Mukarji. P.K., "The Aim of Tribal Education", *Vanyaati* 1960, 9(1), 26-28.

Mukherjee,Alvin J., "Study of Shifting Cultivation: A critical Appraisal", *The Eastern Anthropologist,* 1988, 41 (1), 93-98.

Mukarjee, A.B., "Bhawanti Housetype in Andhra Pradesh", Geographical Journal, 1962, 13.

Mukherjee, B., "Comparative Study of the Kinship System of Six Matrilineal Tribes", *Eastern Anthropologist,* 1961, 14 (3), 216-228.

Mukherjee, Bhadabanda, "The Tribal Amazons in Matrilineal Society", Tribal Women in India, *Indian Anthropological Society.*

Mukherjee, Bhadabanda, "Tribalism and Extremism in Tripura', *Journal of the Indian Anthropological* Society, 1981, 16(2), 145-148.

Mukherjee, B.B., "Dual Organisation Among the Uralis of Travancore", *Vanyajti,* 1954, 2(4).

Mukherjee, B.B., "Garo Family", *Eastern Anthropologist* 1957, 11(!), 25-30.

Mukherjee, B.B., "Machong among the Garos of Assam", *Eastern Anthropologist*1955-56, 9 (2), 112-116.

Mukherjee, B.B., "Marriage among the Kanikkars of Travancore", *Bulletin of Department of Anthropology,* Govt. of India, 1956, 5(1).

Mukherjee, B.B., "Marriage Customs and Kinship Organisation of the Urali of Travancore", *Bulletin of Department of Anthropology* Govt. of India, 1952, 1(2).

Mukherjee, B.B., "Santal in relation to Indian Castes", Man in India, 1960, 40 (4), 300-306.

Mukherjee, B.N., S.K., Das and P. Dara Sharma, " Serum Protein and red cell enzyme polymorphism in Oraon Tribe, India", *Ann Human Biology,* 1975, 2. 201-204.

Mukherjee, D.P., "Some biological dimension of tribal economy in India", *Bulletin of the Dept. of Anthropology*, Dibrugarh Univ. 1978-1979. 7 and 8, 8-16.

Mukherjee, D.P., "Variation in defective colour vision among some tribes of Assam", *Bulletin of the Anthropological Survey of India,* 1963, 12 (1-2), 39-42.

Mukherjee, R.K., "The Khasi Huts of Mawphang", *Anthropology Papers,* 1941, (6), 171-187.

Mutatkar, R.K., "Education in Tribal Setting", *Tribal Research Bulletin,* 1. (2), 16. 1979.

Nag, Amit Kumar, "The Bodo-Kacharis, *North-Eastern Spectrum* Vol. II, September. October. 1977, No. 3-4. pp. 7-11.

Nag, Moni, "Cultural Factors Affecting Family Planning", *Journal of Family Welfare,* No. 21, Vol. 3.

Nag M.K., "A Demographic Study of the Kanikkars of Tranvancore", *Bulletin of the Dept. of* Anthropology, Govt. of India, 1954b, 3 (3).

Nag M.K., "Effects of Christianity on Few Aspects of Khasi Culture", *Bulletin of Anthropological Survey of India,* Vol. XIV, 1965.

Nag M.K., "Family Structure of the Kanikkars and Uralis of Travancore", *Bulletin of the Dept. of Anthropology,* Govt. of India, 1954a 3(3).

Nag M.K., "Facets of Christianity on a Few Aspects of Khasi Culture", *Bulletin of Anthropological; Survey of India,* 1965, 14 (1-2).

Nag M.K., "Family and Marriage in Lahaul Valley" *Eastern Anthropologist,* 1960, 8(8).

Naik, J.P., "Education of Scheduled Castes and Scheduled Tribes", *Report of the Seminar on Employment of Scheduled Castes and tribes,* Manager of Publication, Govt. of India, New Delhi, 1965.

Naik, T.B., "How to Educate Aboriginate", *Indian Journal of Social Work,* 1959, 11(2), 172-180.

Naik, T.B., "Labour Problems of Tribal Gujarat", *Adkhadananda,* December, 1950.

Naik, T.B., "The Turbulent Bhils of Alirajpur", *Bulletin of the Anthropological Society of Bombay,* 1968a.

Nair, S.P., "Problems in Tribal Housing",*Vanyajati,* 1960, 8(2), 48-50.

Nakane, Chie, "The Nayar Family in Disintegrating Matrilineal System", *International Journal of Comparative Sociology,* 1962, 3. 17-28.

Nandi, S., "Plank Press: A Variant", *Bulletin of Anthropological Survey of India,* 1964, 13 (1-2).

Nath, Jogindra., "The Social Ethics of Adi Marriage", *North Eastern Spectrum,* Vol. I September, October. 1976. No. 3 and 4 . pp. 22-25.

Navalakh, S.K., "Authority Structure Among the Bhumij and Bhils : A Study Historical Causation", *Eastern Anthropologist,* 1959, 12 (1).

Needham, R., "A Structural Analysis of Aimol Society", Bijdragen tot de Taal, *Landen Volken unde,* Vol. 116. PP. 81-108, 1960b.

Needham, R., "A Structural Analysis of Purum Society", *American Anthropologist,* Vol. LX, Pp. 75-101. 1958.

Needham, R., "An Analytical Note on the Kom of Manipur", Ethonos, 1959. 24.

Needham, R., "Chowte Social Structure", *American Anthropologist,* 1960. 60.

Needham, R., "Patrilateral Prescriptive Alliance and The Ungarinyin", *Southwestern Journal of Anthropology,* 1959, 15.

Newell, W,H., "Report on Scheduled Castes and Tribes (A Study of Gaddi Scheduled Tribes and Affiliated Castes. *Census of India,* 1961, 20, (pt. VB).HimachalPradesh,Simla,1967.

Newell, W.H., "Goshem: A Gaddi Village in the Himalyaya", in M.N. Srinivas (ed.) *India's Villages,* Asia Publishing House, Bombay, 1960, 56-57.

Nevile and Borodoloi, " Notes on Caste in Frontier Tribes", *Census of India,* 1921, 8. Assam, Pt. I. Govt. Press, Shillong, 1923.

Nijar, Bakhshish Singh, "Women and Social Slavery in Punjab", *Journal of the Indian History,* Vol. LVI. December. 1978., pt. III. Pp. 478-494.

Nibedon, Nirmal., "Strange Stories, of Nagaland", *Eastern Spectrum,* Vol. I May-June, 1927. Nos. 11-12. pp. 21-23.

Nobinchandra, L., "Point of View: Tribes of Mainpur –Its Problems and Perspective", *Resistance*: October 17, 1978. p.3.,

Noble, William A., "Toda Dwellings and Temples", *Anthropos* 1966. 61 (3-6).

Ogle, M.M.J., "Extract from the Narrative Report of Mi. M.J. Ogle, *General Report of the Operations of the Survey of India during 1884-1885,* Appindex, pp. 5-10

Ogle, M.J., "Report of 15th May, 1876, *Gerneral Report of the Topographical Surveys of India, 1875-1876.*, pp. 72-5, on Lhota, Rengma, Sema, Eastern Angamis.

Orans, Martin, "A Tribal People in an Industrial Setting", in Milton Singer (ed.), *Traditional India,* Structure and Change, the American Folklore Society, Philadelphia, 1959, 216-239.

Orans, Martin, "Our Indigenous Peoples – Mao Folk Migration", Resistance : May 11, 1976, p.3.,

Orans, Martin, "Our Indigenous Peoples – The Mao", *Resistance* April, 6, 1976. April, 13, 1976.

Orans, Martin, "Our Indigenous Peoples – The Kabui", *Resistance*: April 27, 1976, pp. 327. May, 4, 1976, p. 4.

Orans, Martin, "Our Indigenous Peoples – The Korieng-Origin and Migration", *Resistance*: August 10, 1976, pp. 3-4. August 17, 1976, pp. 3-4.

Pabla, G.S., and Vashistha, J.R., "Tandi: A village in Lahual and Spiti District of Punjab State", *Census of India*, 1961, 13(1), (Part-IV), Village Survey, Monograph No. 1 Manager of Publications, Delhi, 1963.

Pakrasi, K., " Some Aspects of Tribal Education", Vanyajati, 1956, 4(4). 127-133.

Pandit, T.N., "Tribes of Andaman and Nicobar Islands", K.S. Singh (ed.), *Tribal Situation in India*, 1988.

Paranavitana, S., "Matrilineal Descent in the Sinhalese Royal Family", *Cylon Journal of Science* (Section A), Vol. II.

Pascoe, E.H., "A Traverse Across the Naga Hills of Assam from Dimapur to the Neigbourhood of Seramati Peak", *Records of the Geological Survey of India,* Cal. XLII. October.4. (1912). Pp. 236-64.

Patel, M.L., "Agro-Economic Problems of Tribals of India" in Budhadeb Chanudhuri (ed.), *Tribal Development in India*, Inter-India Publications, New Delhi, 1982.

Patel, M.L., "Economic Constraints of the Development", Seminar *Papers on Strategies for Tribal Development,* J.N.K. University, Jabalpur, 1979.

Patel, M.L., "Farm Investment Pattern of the Tribal Village in Madhya Pradesh", *Indian Journal of Agriculatural Economics,* Bombay, 1965.

Patel, M.L., "Integrated Area Development with Special Reference to Mandla", *Bulletin of the Tribal Research Institute*, Bhopal, 1972.

Patel, M.L., "Investment in Human Resources in Tribal Village of Madhya Pradesh", Paper Read at the *Indian Economic Conference*, Banaras, 1965.

Patel, M.L., " Micro-Planning for Human Resources Development in Tribal Area of Madhya Pradesh", *M.P. Economic*

Patel, M.L., "Planning for Tribal Development in Madhya Pradesh", *Man and Life,* 1980.

Patel, M.L., "Some Aspects of Educational Development of Tribals", *Bulletin of Cultural Research Institute,* Calcutta, 1974.

Patel, M.L., "Spatial Mobility of Educated Tribes of Mandala Districts", *Vanyajati,* Quaterly New Delhi, 1970.

Patel, M.L., "Tribal Development Through the Approach in Fourth Plan", *Khadi Gramodyog Journal,* Bombay, 1967.

Pathak, K.B., "Observations on 'Open Birth Interval and Open Status' as Indicators of Fertility Changes", *Journal of Family Welfare'* March, 1970.

Pathak, Leela, "Sterilizing the Women" *Yojana*, 15 September. 1968

Patnaik, N. "An Apprisal of Ashram School Education", *Report of the Fourth Conference of Tribesf and Tribes Area,* 1957.

Paul, Madam C., "Bodo-Kachari: Toiling Plains Tribals of the Brahmaputra Valley", *The Quarterly Review of Historical Studies,* (Pub. By the Institute of Historical Studies, 35. Theatre Road. Calcutta – 700 017), Vol. XXIII No. I 1983-84. pp. 30-35.

Pawsey, C.R., "Folk Tales from the Naga Hills", *Folk-lore* Vol. XXXIII (1922), pp. 397-405. 2 Vols. XXXIV (1923). Pp. 235-5. Euroneously ascribed to J.H. Hutton. Angami Naga Tales.

Peal, S.E., "Eastern Nagas of Tirp and Namstick", JASB Calcutta Vol. LXN-1896).

Peal, S.E., "Naga Method of Climbing Large Trees", *Proceddings of the Asiatic Society of Bengal* (1872), pp. 135-8.

Peal, S.E., "On Some Traces of the Kol-Mon-Anam in the Eastern Naga Hills", *Journal of the Asiatic Society of Bengal,* Vol. LXV (1896), pp. 20-4.

Peal, S.E., "On the 'Morong' and other Customs of the Natives of Assam", *British Association for the Advancement of Science*, 1892, pp. 801-2.

Peal, S.E., "The Communal Barracks of Primitive Races, *Journal of the Asiatic Society of Bengal*, Vol. LXI, pt. 2 (1892), pp. 168-82.

Peal, S.E., "The Nagas and Neighbouring Tribes", *Journal of the Anthropological Institute,* Vol. III, 1874, pp. 476-81.

Peter, Prince, "Possible Survivals of Toda Rituals", *Bulletin of Madras Govt. Museum,* 1953. b. 6(1).

Peter, Prince, "The Todas, Some Additions and Corrections to W.H.R. Rivers Book Observed in the Field", *Man*, 1955, 4.

Peter, Prince, "The Problem of Toda Survival", *Vanyajati,* 1953a, 1(3). 59-68.

Pethe, Vasant P., "Poverty and Many Children as Causes of Inadequate Nourishment and Upbringing of Children *Journal of Family Welfare,* June, 1961.

Pettigrew, W. "Kathi Kasham", *Journal of the Royal Asiatic Society of Bengal,* Vol. V, 1909, pp. 37-46.

Piggott, Stuart, "Nomad House Sites in the Western Himalayas", *Man* 1944. 44 (121).

Prasad, Saileswar, " Education of Scheduled Tribes and Nomads", in L.P. Vidhyarthi and B.N. Sahay (ed.) *Applied Anthropology and Development in India*, National Publishing House, New Delhi, 1980.

Prasad, S.D., "Jojohatu: A Munda Village", (Bihar Village Survey Monograph No. 1). *Census of India 1961,*Manager of Publications, Delhi, 1963.

Radclifffe-Brown, A.R., "The Relationship System of the Dieri Tribes", *Man*, Vol. XIV, No. 33, pp.53-6, 1914.

Radcliffe-Brown, A.R., "Three Tribes of Western Austraila", *Journal of the Royal Anthropological Institute,* Vols. XLIII, pp. 143-70, 1913.

Raju, P.S.S., "The Religious belers of Koyas as Described in Koya Folk tales", *The Eastern Anthropologist*, 1988, 41 (1), 99-102.

Ramesh, A., N.M., Blake, M. Bijaya Kumar and J.S. Murthy, "Genetic Studies on the Chenchu Tribe of Andhra Pradesh", *Human Heredity*, 1980, 30, 29-198.

Ramasubhan, Radhika, "The Naga Impasse in India", *The Eastern Anthropologist,* Vol. 31. No. 4. October – December 1978, pp. 393-412.

Ramkrishnan, P.S., "Tribal man in the Jumid tropics of the North-East", *Man in India*, Vol. 65, No. !. March 1985, pp.1-32.

Rana, Manish Kumar, "A Note on Changes in the Magico Religious Befiefs and Practices of the Oraons", Bulletine of the Cultural Research Institute, 1962, 1 (2).

Ranade, R.M. "Oil Pressing as Home Industry among the Bhils and Bhilalas", *Vanyajati*, 1956, 4. 40-41.

Rao (B. Janardhan) and Babu (P. Narendra), "Nehru and Tribal Policy of Intergration", *Mainstream,* November, 12, 1988, pp. 54-56.

Rao, C.H., "Mysore Castes and Tribes A General Survey", *Quartely Journal of Mythilic Society,* 1922-23, 13.

Rao, M.S.A., "Sociology of North Eastern Hill Areas", *Proceedings of the Third Summer School Kohima, April 7-14,* Dept. of Sociology and Centre of Advanced Study, University of Delhi, 1970.

Rao, Y. Sudharshan, "Tribal Resistance to Imperialism with Regerence to Totapalli Affair Andhra Pradesh", *Indian History* Congress, Vol. I. 47th Session, Srinagar, 1986, 567-570.

Rashna, S.N., Mahakud N.K., "The Kishan Children at Work: Data from a West Orissa", *Man in India,* 1988, 68(4), 369-379.

Rawal, I.B., "A Study of Crime Among the Bhils", *Man in India,* July-September. 1964.

Rawlins, J., "On the Manner, Religion and Laws of the Kukis", *Asiatic Researchers,* 2:187-93, 1807.

Ray, Nihar Ranjan, "Introductory Address", *The Tribal Situation in India,* K.S. Singh (ed.), Indian Institute of Advanced Study.

Ray, P.C., "The Effect of Culture – Contact on the Personality Structure of Two Indian Tribes The Riang of Tripura and Baija of M.P.", *Bulletin of Anthropological Survey of India,* 1957, 6(2), 1-84.

Ray, P.C., "The Tensional Feelings Among the Abors and Gallong as Indicated by Rorschach Technique", *Indian Journal of Psychology,* 1955, 30 (Part-I), 95-103.

Read, C.H., "Naga Ornaments", *Journal of the Anthropological Institute,* Vol. XiX, 1891, p. 441.

Reddy, A.P. and B.N. Mukherjee, "A Brief Study of Nomadic Tribe: Kuruvikharans of Andhra Pradesh and Tamil Nadu", *Journal of the Anthropological Society,* 1981, 16(2), 179-184.

Rohini, A., "Some Demographic Trends Among the Tribal Women of Andhra Pradesh", *Man and Life,* 1987. 13 (1 and 2), 91-96.

Rongmuthu, D.S., "Legends of Supreme Sacrifice as Reflected through the Garo Folk-lore", *North Eastern Spectrum,* Vol. 11 August. 1977, ano. 2, pp. 10-15.

Rongmuthu, D.S., "Mantras and Mantric Process", *North Eastern Spectrum* Septemebr-October 1977, No. 3 and 4, pp. 32-41.

Rongmuthu, D.S., "Marriage and Customs of Garos", *North Eastern Spectrum,* Vols. II, March-May, 1978. No. 9-11. pp. 13-16.

Rongmuthu, D.S., "Nokpande – The Bachelors' Dormitory", *North Eastern Spectrum,* Vol. I, Novermber 1976, No. 5, pp. 57-61.

Rongmuthu, D.S., "Wan gala – The Harvest Festival of the Garos", *North Eastern Spectrum,* Vol. I, May-June, 1977, Nos. 11-12, pp. 9-20.

Rosser, Colin, "A Hermit Village in Kulu", in M.N. Srinivas (ed.) *Indias Villages,* Asia Publishing House, Bombay, 1960, 77-90.

Rosner, Victor, "Tribal Drums", *Man of India,* 1955, 7. 26-29.

Rout, S.P., "Social Orgaizat:on of the Bhuiyas of Kolanandi", 1967-68, 9(1), 50-58.

Rout, S.P., "Social Organization of the Bhuiyas of Kolanandi", *Adivasi* 1967-68, 9(1), 50-58.

Rout, S.P., "Socio-Economic Impilactions of Pus Puni Rituals of the Hill Juang of Keonjnar", *Adivasi,* 1966-67, 8.

Rout, S.P., "The Juang and Culture Change", *Adivasi,* 1966-67, 8(1), 23-28.

Roy, Burman, B.K. "Post Primitives of Chota Nagpur: *Race and Society,* Paris, UNESCO, 1979.

Roy, Burman, B.K. "A Note on the Progress of Secor .ary Education Among the Scheduled Castes and the Schedul· Tribes of West Bengal", *Bulletion of the lcultural Research . stitute,* 1966, 5 (1-2), 59-66.

Roy, Burman, B.K. "Chetlat: An Island in a Arabian Sea", *Census of India* I Offices of the Registrar General, New Delhi, 1970 c. (Monograph No. 3).

Roy, Burman, B.K. "Comparative Study of the Progress of Secondary Education among the Scheduled Castes and Scheduled Tribes of West Benfal", *Bulletin of the Cultural Research Institute,* 1963 b. 2(1), 40-52.

Roy, Burman, B.K. "Forests and Tribals in India", in L.P. Vidyarthi (ed.), *Applied Anthropology in India,*Kitab Mahal, Allahabad, 1968.

Roy, Burman, B.K. "Integrated Area Approach to the Problems of the Hill Tribes of North-East India", in *Tribal Situation in India,* K.S. Singh (ed.) Indian Institute of Advanced Study, Simla, 1972.

Roy, Burman, B.K. "Issues in Land Reforms in North East Tribal Area – I and II", *Mainstream*, Vols. XXV, Nos. 46. August.1, 1987 and Vol. XXV, Nos. 47, August *, 1987.

Roy, Burman, B.K. "Meaning and Process of Tribal Integration in a Democratic Society",*Sociological Bulletin,* 1961, 10(1), 27-41.

Roy, Burman, B.K. "Modernization Process in the Bhils of North East India", *Journal of the Institute of Defence Strategy,* 1970a, Mim.

Roy, Burman, B.K. "Problems of Tribal Language in Education", *Vidyapith,* October 18 1965, 18-22.

Roy, Burman, B.K. "Relative Roles of Government and Voluntary Agencies in Education of Tribal People", *Report of the Nationa Seminar on Tribal Education in India,* NCERT, New Delhi, 1967m 121-132.

Roy, Burman, B.K. "Strategies of Tribal Development", in L.P. Vidyarthi (ed.), *Tribal Development and Its Administration,* New Delhi, Concept Publishing Company, 1981.

Roy, Burman, B.K. "Structure of Bridge and Buffers Communities in the Border Aread", *Man in India,* 1966, 46(2) 103-107.

Roy, Burman, B.K. "The Birnors", *Bulletin of the Cultural Research Institute,* 1964, a, 3(1), 19-30.

Roy, Burman, B.K., "Transformation of Tribes and Analogous Social Formations", *Econimic and Polotical Weelky,* 1983, XVIII (27), 1172-1174.

Roy, Burman, B.K., "The Manalis", Bullentin of the Culture *Research Indistute,* 1963 a, (3), 31-32.

Roy, Burman, B.K., "Tribal Demography in India – A Preliminary Apprisal (Read in Seminar on Tribal Situation in India), I.I.A.S., Simla, 1969.

Roy, Burman, J.J., "Clan, Age-grade and Role of the aged in an Ao-Naga Village", *Journal of the Indian Anthropological Soceity,* 1987, 22(2-3), 281.

Roy, Nilima, "Basketry and Domestic Utnesils of Asia", *Vanyajati,* 1955 5(4), 170-174.

Roy, Nilima, "Habitations of the Adis of the Siang Frontier Division", *Vanyajati,* 1957b. 5, 125-133.

Roy, P.C., "The Manual Ability of the Kanikkar of Travancore "*Bulletin of the Dept. of Anthropology,* Govt. of India, 1955, 4(1).

Roy, R.C., "Note on the Chawte Kuki Clan", *Man in India,* 1936, 16(1).

Roy, Sachin, "Abor Weapons of War and Chase", *Journal of the Asiatic Society,* 1956, 22(2), 139-159.

Roy, Sachin, "Dress Ornaments and Decoration of the Asia of NEFA", *Vanyajati,* 1956, 22(2).

Roy, Sachin, "Hunting and Fishing Among the Adis", *Vanayjati,* 1958, 6(2), 140-152.

Roy, S.C., "The Black Bhils of Jaisamaond Lake in Rajputan", *Journal of Bihar and Orissa Research Society*, 1924, 10.97-113.

Roy, Shivani and S,H,M, Rizvi, "Tribal Hillucinogenic Tradition: A Case Study of Manipur Village", *Man in India*, Vols, 67. No.2, June 1987, pp. 137-147.

Roy, S.C., "The Nagas, the Kascharis and the Meities: Their Affinity with Chota Nagpur Tribes", *Man in India,* Vol. 61, 1981, p. 293.

Roy, S.K., "A Note on Carpentary Tools (Rua.), Eastern Garo Hills, Meghalaya", *Bulletin of the Dept. of Anthropology, Dibrugarh* University, 1986, 9. 202-205.

Roychoudhury, A.K., "Gene Differntiation Among Six Tribes in Bihar", *Journal of the Indian Anthropological Society*1986, 13.287-291.

Ruhela, Satyapal, "Gaduliya Lohar", *Tribe,* 1967, 3(2), 1-14.

Ruhela, S.P., "Some Educational Problems of Scheduled Tribes in Rajasthan", *Jan Jagriti,* 1964. 2(1).

Roy, G.S., "A Few Folk Songs of the Adivasis of Kolhau", *Man in India,* 1949, 29. 172-174.

Sachidanada, 'Socio-Economic Aspects of Tribal Education', *Report of the National Seminar on Tribal Education in India*, N.C.E.R.T., New Delhi, 1967, 99-108.

Sachidanada, 'Tribal Education in India', *Vanyajati,* 1964, 12(1), 3-6.

Sachidanada, 'Economic Development, Education and Social Change in Arunachal', *Man in India,* Col.65. No. 1 March, 1985.

Sah, Vimal, 'Tribal Education in Gujarat', *Vanyajati,* 1966, 14 (3), 109-112.

Saha, N., 'Customs and Economy: A Study of Shifting Cultivation in North Eastern India', S.M., Dubey (ed.) *North East India: A Sociological Study,* Concept Publishing House, Delhi, 1983.

Sahay, K.N., 'A Study in Process of Tranformation from Tribe to Caste : Parabiyas of Lolki A Case Study', Journal of Social Research, 1967, 10(1), 64-89.

Sahay, K.N., 'Trends of Sanskritisation among the Oraon', *Bulletion of Bihar Tribal Research Institute,* 1962, 4(2).

Sahay, K.N., 'Impact of Christianity on the Oraon of three Villages in Chotanagpur', (Doctoral Thesis, Ranchi Univ. Unpub.), 1964.

Saikia, P.D., 'Village Leadership in North East India', *Man in India,* Vol.43, 1963, p.192.

Samanta, R.K., 'Note on Hill Tribes of North East India', *Man in India,* Vol. 60, 1980, p. 129.

Samanta, R.K., Socio-Agro-Economic Characteristics of Modern Agricultural Technology', *J.N.E. Indian Council for Social Science Research,* 1979, 3(2), 1-5.

Samanta, R.K., and Adhikari, M.M., "Marriage Systems Among Tribals of North East India', *Man in India* 1988, 68(4), 401-412.

Samanta, R.K. and M. Narasimha Reddy, 'Koya of Andhra and their Socio-Psychological and Agro-Economic Characteristics', *Journal of the Indian Anthropological Society,* 1982, 17 (3), 229-234.

Samuell, E.A., Notes on a Forest Race called Putto or Juang', *Journal of the Asiatic Society of Bengal,* 1856, 25, 295-363.

Sandhwar, A.N., 'The Method of Christian Conversion among the Tribals:The Korwa Convert Palaman', *Journal of Social Research,* 1973 16(1).

Sanwal, R.D., 'Study of Social Stratification in the Hill Regions of Uttar Pradesh', in Beharilal Abbi and Satish Sabarwal (eds.) *Urgent Research in Social Anthropology,* Indian Institute of Advanced Study, Simla, 1969.

Sanyal, Shubhendu, 'Primitive Tribe of Bihar :Strategy for Development", *Man in India.* 1968, 68(4), 356-368.

Saran A.B., 'Murder and suicide Among the Tribes of Chotanagpur' (Doctoral Dissertation), Ranchi Univ. Unpub. 1961.

Sarkar, Jayanta, 'Extent of Tribal Involvment in Rajputaisation Process:A case study in Western Mandhya Pardesh', *Journal of the Indian Anthropological Society,* 1981, 16 (1), 51-58.

Sarkar, Sasanka, 'The Malers of the Rajamahal Hills', *Man in India,* 1933, 13.

Sastri, V.N.V.K., 'Two Raj-Gond Uprisings in Forty Years: A conflict Analysis', *Man and Life,* 1984, 10 (1and 2), 62-76.

Sen, J., 'Problems in Tribal Transformation', *Man in India,* 1966, 46.

Sen, J., 'The Jharkhand Movement' in *Tribal Situation in India,* K.S. Singh (ed.) Indian Institute of Advanced study, Simla, 1972.

Sen, Ranjan Kumar, 'Changing Population Growth Rate : Its Effect on Per Capita National Income', *Economic Weekly,* 1st November. 1958.

Sengupta, N.K., 'A Note on the 'survey and Investigation on some Physical Conditions and Nutrition Patterns in relation to the Tribal People in Singhbhum, *Man in India,* 1988, 68(4), 473-476.

Sengupta, P.N., 'The Investigation into the Deitary, Habit of the Aborigional Tribes of Abor Hills, Bulletine of Anthropological Survey of India, 1954, 3(2) and 1955, 4(2).

Sengupta, P.N., 'Investigation into the Deitary Nutrition of Nocte Tribe of Tirap Frontier Division of NEFA', Bulletion of Deptt. of Anthropology,1960. 9(2), 25-38.

Sengupta, S., 'A Note on Nage Anthropometry, *Journal of the Asiatic Society of Bengal,* Vol. XVII, 1951, pp. 1-5

Sengupta, Sabuj and Pathak S., 'A Study on Sexual Maturation in the Tribal (Kole) giral of Koteswar-Marwa Region of Madhya Pradesh', *Man in India,* 1988, 68(4) 470—472.

Bevak, Ram, 'Adivasi Movement in Chotanagpur', *The Quarterly Review of Historical Studies,* Vol. XXII, (1982-83), July-September-November. 2 p. 35-39.

Shadwell, 'Note on the inhabitants of the Khasi and Jaintia Hills, *Journal of the Asiatic Society of Bengal,* Vol. IX, 1840.

Shah, P.G., 'Bhils the Earliest Inhabitants of Gujarat', *Journal of the Gujarat Research Soceity,* 1939, 1(4).

Shah, P.G., 'Education and Social change Among Tribals in *Indian Sociological Bulletin,* 28 (1-2) 1979, 25-45.

Shah, P.G., 'Non-Hindu Elements in the Culture of the Bhils of Gujarat', In J.P. Mills and others (eds.) *Essays in Anthropology Presented to Rai Bahadur S.C. Roy,* Maxwell and Co. Lucknow, 1942, 164-186.

Shaiza, Rano, M., 'Point of View-Nagaland Today', *Resistance,* June 28, 1977, p. 3. July 5, 1977, pp. 3-4.

Shakerspear, J., 'Southern Tangkul Notes', *Man in India,* Vol. XII, No. 50, 1912.

Shakerspear, J., 'Tangkhul Folk Tales and Notes on Some Festivals of the Hills Tribes South of Assam', *Flok-Lore,* Vol. XXXIII, 1922, pp. 265-81.

Shakerspear, J., 'Manipur Festivals' *Folk-lore XXII, 1910. 79-82.*

Shakerspear, J., 'Manipur Proverbs', *Folk-lore XXII,* 1911, 473-475.

Shakerspear, J., 'Notes on the Iron-workers of Manipur and Annual Festival in honour of their special deity Kunulanba', *Journal of Royal Anthropological Insititue, 1910.40.*

Shakerspear, J., 'The Pleasing of God Thangjing', *Man,* 1913, 13

Shakerspear, J., 'The Customs of Death among the Manipuris and Congnate Clans, *Folklore,* Vol. 21, London, 1912.

Shangkham, G., *'A Brief Account of the Moyons'*, unpub. 1987.

Hingham, G., 'British Policy Towards the Nagas – 1834-1880, (Unpub) M. Phil Dissertation of J.N.U., New Delhi, 1979.

Sharma, B.D., 'An Approach to the Development of Onges of Little Andaman', *Journal of Social Research,* 1976, 19(2).

Sharma,B.S.K., 'Shifting Cultivation (Jhuming), in Manipur and Nagaland Region', *Manipur Today*, Govt. of Manipur, Directorate of Information and Public Relations, Jan., 1981, Vol. I.

Sharma, Gyaneswar, 'Point of View-Tea Cultivation in Manipur', *Resistance*, August, 31, 1976. p. 31.

Sharma, K.K., 'Boro-Kachari Kinship terms-A Preliminary Note', *Bulletin of the Deptt. Of Anthropology*, Dibrugarh Univ. 1978-79, 7and8, 123-131.

Sharma, T.R., 'Primary Education in Ranchi Tribal Village', *Bulletin of Bihar Research Institute,* 1962, 4(1), 76-89.

Sharma,V.D., 'Tribal Education in Rajasthan', *Journal of the Tribal Research Institute and Training Centre,* 1966, 2(1-2), 1-4).

Shatapathy, Digambar, 'Roal of Tribal Youth in Tribal Development', *Khadi Gramodyog,* A monthly Journal, Khadi and Village Industry Commission, Bombay, April, 1984.

Shegal, John., 'Habits' Manners of the Marvar Tribes of India', *Memoir of the Anthropological Society* of London, 1867-69, 3. 201-216.

Shrikant, L.M., 'Education Commission and Backward Classes', *Vanyajati,* 1966b, 15(3), 128-30.

Shrikant, L.M., 'Measures Proposed for the Spread of Education Among the Scheduled Tribes', *Vanyajati,* 1966a, 15(3), 133-138.

Shyamchoudhuri, N.K., 'The Stone Pottery of Manipur and Its Cultural Significance', *Bulletin of Anbthropological Survey of India,* 1962. 11 (3-4).

Shymalal, 'Planting A Misssion Among the Bhils of South Rajasthan', *Man and Life*, 1984, 10 (1and2), 77-96.

Singh, Banvir, 'Political Organistion of North Indian Tribe', *Eastern Anthropologist,* 1969, 22(3).

Singh, B.B., 'Land Use, Cropping Pattern and their Ranking' *National Grographical Journal of India,* Vol. 13, pt. 1, 1967.

Singh, Chongtham, 'Our Indigeneous People-The Purum', Resistance, January 11, 1977, p. 3. January 18, 1977, pp. 3-4.

Singh, G.P., 'The Genesis and Growth of Tribal Civilization in North India', *The Quarterly Review of Historical Studies,* Vol. XX, 1980, No.4. Institute of Historical Studies, Calcutta, pp. 13-18.

Singh, G.P., 'The Genesis and Growth of Tribal Civilization in North India', *The Quarterly Review of Historical Studies*, Vol. LVII, Auguest, December 1979, Parts II and III. Pp. 189-198.

Singh, Inder, P. 'Tribes of Manipur', *Kurukshetra,* A Fortnightly Journal, July, 1977, 16-31.

Singh, Jasbir, 'Optimum carring', *Kurukshetra,* A Fortnightly Journal, July, 1977, 16-31.

Singh, Jasbir, 'Optimum carrying capacity of land, Caloric density and intensisty of Population pressure changes in Punjab, 1951-61, *The National Geographical Journal of India*, Vol. XVII, pt. I, 1971.

Singh, J.P., 'Pattern of Land use in Urban areas: A Case study of Shillong, *Indian Geographical Studies Bulleting,* No. 6, 1976.

Singh, K.B., 'Festivals of Manipur', *Akashvani,* 1966, 31(48).

Singh, K.B., 'Manipur Vaishnavism', *Sociological Bulletin*, 1963, 12. Bomaby.

Singh, K.B., 'A Profile of Meitel Culture', *Bharat Sewak,* 1964, 11 (4).

Singh, K.B., 'Men and Women of Manipur' *Akashvani*, 32(38), 1967.

Singh, K.B., 'Salvery in Manipur', *Folk-lore XVIII,* 1975, 7-9.

Singh, K.B., 'Traces of Pre-Hinduism in the Meitei Soceity' *Folk-lore,* Calcutta, 1964, 5(6)

Singh, K.B., 'Women of Manipur', *Trend Bombay,* 1961, 10(10).

Singh, K.S., 'Agraian Issues in Chotanagpur', in *Tribal Situation in India* K.S. (ed.) Indian Institute of Advanced Study, Simla, 1972.

Singh, K.S., 'Incidence of colour blindness among Tangkhul Naga of Manipur', *Journal of the Anthropological Society,* 1982, 17 (1), 79-82.

Singh, K.S., 'Transformation of Tribal Society: Integration vs. Assimilation', *EPW,* Bombay. Vol. XVII.No. 34, August. 1966, 31(48).

Singh, M.Bokul, 'Death and Disposal in the Maram Tribes of Manipur', *Bulletin of the Deptt. of* Anthropology, Dibrugarh, Vol. 16-17 (1987-88). Pub. In 1991.

Singh, M.Bokul, 'The Marams of Manipur : An Ethnographic Study', Centre for Tribal Studies, M.U, 1991.

Singh,N.R., ' Marriage by Elopment among the Meiteis of Manipur', *Man in India,* LIII, 1973, 2. 135-152.

Singh, R.K. Ranjit, 'The Glimpse of the Monsang Culture and History' (mineogrpahy) *The Monsang Historical and Customary Research Committee, 1978.*

Singh, R.K. Ranjit and Bhagabati Ananda, 'The Monsang of Monsang of Manipur: A Preliminary report on identity Orientation, *Bulletin of the Deptt. of Anthropology,* Dibrugarh Univ. 1980. 97-85.

Singh, S.J., 'Habitation on the Meiteies', *Man in India,* 1933, 13.

Singh, S.J., The Meitei Calendar', *24th Indian Science Congress,* 1937.

Singh,Yogendra, 'A Note on Cultural Integration on Tribal Soceity in India', *Tribe,* 1968, 2(1-3), 13-16.

Sinha, D.P., 'Innovation, Response and Development in Bonari', *Man in India,* 1968a. 48(3). 225-242.

Sinha, D.P., 'A Profile of Meitei Culture', *Bharat Sewak,* 1964, 11(4).

Sinha, Surjit, 'State Formation and Rajpur in Tribal Central India', *Man in India,* 1962, 42(1), 35-80.

Sinha, Surjit, 'Tribal Culture of Peninsular India: Dimension of little Tradition in Study of Indian Civilization', *Man in India*, 1975a, 37(2), 93-118.

Sinha, Surjit, 'Tribal Cultures of Peninsular India: Dimension of little Tradition in Study of Indian Civilization', A Preliminary statement', *Journal of American Folk-lore,* 1958, 71(279), 504-518.

Sinha, Surjit, 'Tribes and Indian Civilization : A perspective', *Man in India,* 1880-60.

Sinha, Surjit, ' Tribal Solidarity Movements in India: A review in *Tribal Situation in India,* K.S., Singh (ed.) Indian Institute of Advanced Study, Simla, 1972.

Sinha, S.C., 'Tribal Societies in India: Case for Development through Conservation', *Conservation of Natutre,* Calcutta, 1984.

Sinha, T.C., 'The Psyche of the Garos', *Anthropological Survey of India,* Calcutta, 1966.

Siodia, V.N., 'Three Styles in Architecture of Varti Dwellings', *Anthropos* 1964, 59(1-2), 159-169.

Smith, W.C., 'Ao Naga Folk-Tales', *Folk-lore,* Vol. XXXVI, 1926, pp. 371-94.

Smith, W.C., 'Missionary Activities and The Acceleration of Backward Proples', *Journal of Applied Sociology*, Vol. VII 1923, 175-86.

Soletore, S.N., 'The Bhils of Maharastra', *New Indian Anthropology,* 1938.

Som, R.K., 'Demographic Factors in Planning for Economic and Social Development in African Countries', in Ashish Bose et al (ed.) *Studeis in Demography*, Grorge Allen and Unwin Ltd. London, 1970.

Somasekhar, A., 'Tribal Development in Andhra Pradesh Certain Issues, *Man and Life*, 1987, 13 (1and2) 67-76.

Sorely, H.T., 'Note on the Aborigional and Hill Tribe Found in the Bombay Presidency', *Census of India*, 1931, pt. IIIB, Ministry of Home Affairs, New Delhi, 1935.

Srinivashna, K., 'Demographic Pressure in India and Methods of Control', *Journal of Family Welfare,* September 1960.

Srivastva, L.R.N., 'Some Aspects of Integration of the Tribal People', *Report of the Symposium on Problems of Education of the Tribal People of India,* N.C.E.R.T., New Delhi, 1967b. 77-97.

Srivastva, L.R.N., 'Some Basic Problems of the Tribal People', *Report of the Naional Seminars on Tribal Education in India,* N.C.E.R.T., New Delhi, 1967b. , 77-97.

Srivastava, S.K.,. 'Directed Cultural Change among the Tharus', *Agra University's Journal of Research,* 1956, 4.

Srivastava, S.K., 'Some Problems of Culturall Contacts among the Tharus', *Eastern Anthropologist,* 1949 3(1), 36-39.

Sten, H.W., 'The Behdeinkhlam Festival of the Jaintias' *North Eastern Spectrum,* Vol. 28, 1948, p. 172.

Stonor, C.R., 'Ancestral Ornaments of the Lhota Nagas' *Man in India,* Vol. 28. XLX. 1960.

Stonor, C.R., 'The Feast of Merit among the Northern Sangtam Tribe of Assam', *Anthropos,* Vol. XLX. 1950.

Stonor, C.R., 'The Kejii or Iron Hoe of the Angami Naga', *Man,* 1949, 49 (177).

Stonor, C.R., 'Development of Local Arts and Crafts : A Case Study of Sikkim', *Journal of Himalayan Studies and Regional Development,* 1984, 7and8, 73-80.

Stonor, C.R., 'Tribal Handicrafts of Sikkim: A Profile', *Man in India,* 1988, 68(4), 431-441.

Suguna, A.V.Kiran, A. and Rajpramukh, K.E., 'The Role of Descent groups among the Mannedoras (Andhra Pradesh), *Man in India,* 1988, 68(4), 454-458.

Suman Sao, S.K. Mishra and R.N. Chottopadhyay, 'A Model of Tribal Industrial Growth: Case Study of Rope Making', *Man and Life* 1985, 11(3and4), 207-220.

Swaminathan, M.C. et.al. 'Natrition of the People of Ankote Taluka', North Karala, *Indian Journal of Medical Research.*

Swanton, J.R., 'The Social Organization of American Tribes', *American Anthropologist,* Vol. VII, pp. 663-73, 1905a.

Tanquist, J.E., "The Calendar of the Angami Nagas", *Man in India,* Vol. VII, 1927, pp. 263-76.

Temple, R.C., "Ossuary Feast of Cat Nicobar", *Census of India,* 1901, 3. Supplt. Govt. Printing Press, Cal. 1903a, Part I Report, Appendix B, 226-229.

Teehuja, Khrieteno, "The Christian Church Among the Angami Nagas" in Suresh Singh (ed.) *Tribal Situation in India,* Simla, India Institute of Advanced Study, 1972.

Teehuja, Khrieteno, "The Nagas: A General View", *North Eastern Spectrum*, Vol. II, July-September 1978. No. 1-3. p. 19-22.

Thane, G.D., "On some Naga Skulls", *Journal of the Anthropological Institute,* Vol. XI (18882).

Thanga, Lal Biak, "The Mizos", *North-Eastern Spectrum,* Vol. II, July, 1917, No. I, pp. 29-37.

Thangchungnunga, "The Agricultual Profile in Mizoram", *Journal of North Eastern Council,* January-April, 1986. Vol. VII, No. 1-4.

Thangzawana, R.L., "Mizoram: The Land its People", *North Eastern Spectrum,* I, July, 1976, No. 1, pp. 31-34.

Thungdim, Ngulkhohao, "Point of View-A Danger to Indegenous People", *Resistance,* August. 24, 1976, p. 3. March 29, 1977, pp. 3-4.

Thounaojam, Tarunkumar, "Our Indigenous Proples-Inpresseions of the Tribals of Tripura", *Resistance,* March 22, 1977, p. 3. March 29, 1977, pp. 3-4.

Thurston, E., "Badagas and Irulas of Niligiris: Raniyanas of Malabar; Chinese-Tamil Cross", Summary of Results", *Bulletin of Madras, Govt. Museum,* 1897. 2(2) IV, 1-68.

Thurston, E., "Anthropology of the Todas and Kotas of the Nilgiri Hills : and of Brahmans, Kammalans, Pallis and Pariahs of Madras City", *Bulletin of Madras Govt. Museum,* 1896, 1(4), 139-239.

Thurston, E., "Caste and Tribes of Southern India", 1909, V.

Trail, G.W., "Statistical Sketch of Kumaon", *Asiatic Researches,* 1928, 16.

Trail, G.W., "Tribal Balance Sheet", *Resistance*, Dec. 26, 1978, p. 5.

Trail, G.W., "Tribal Research and Training Institute, *Rajasthan Ke Bhil,* Rajasthan Adminjati Granthmala, No. !, Rajasthan, !965. (Hindi).

Trail. G.W., "Tribal Travesties", *Resistance,* June 14, 1977, p. 5.

Trail, G.W., "Tribal Lands and 20 Point", *Resistance,* July 6, 1976, p. 4.

Tripathi, C.B., "Approaches to Tribal Development and Experience : General Policies, Aministration Approach and Personnel Policies and Their implementation _ An All India Review", *Man in India,* Vol.68, No.4, December 1988, p. 225.

Tripathi, C.B., "Approaches to Tribal Development and Experience : General Policies, Aministrative Approach and Personnel Policies and Their implementation _ An All India Review", *Man in India,* 1988, 68(4), 335-355.

Turner, A.C., "Caste in the Kumaon Division and Tehri Gartiwal State" *Census of India,* 1931.

Turner, A.C., "Caste in the Kumaon Division and Tehri Gartwal State", *Census of India 1931,* Government Press, Simila, 1931.

Venkatesan, D., "Innovations and Their Impact on the Onge of Little Andaman", *Man in India,* 1988, 68(4), 413-423.

Vickers, A., "Among the Nagas", *Blackwood's Magazine,* Vol. CCXVI (1924), pp. 121-9.

Vidyanath, V., "Circular House Type in Kolleru Lake Island (Andhra Pradesh)", *Indian Geographical Journal,* 1962, 37 (2).

Vidyarthi, L.P., "Aspects of Tribal Labour Force in Chhattisgrah", *Tribe,* 1969, 6(3).

Vidyarthi, L.P., "Cultural Change in the Tribes of Modern India", *Journal of Social Research,* 1968a, 11(1), 1-36.

Vidyarthi, L.P., "Education in Tribal Bihar", *Man in India,* 1955, 35(1), 39-45.

Vidyarthi, L.P., "Ranchi Tribals in Andaman and Nicobar Islands", *Searchilight,* April, 1971b.

Vidyarthi, L.P., "Notes on Andaman and Nicobar Islands", *Totus Home,* 1971a 3(1), 30-31.

Vidyarthi, L.P., "Tribal Ethnography in India: A Study of Research in Sociology and Social Anthropology" Vol. III, *Indian Council of Social Science Research,* Popular Prakashan, Bombay, 1972.

Vyas, A.N., "Tribal Education in Orissa", *Report of the 2nd Conference for Tribes and Tribal (Secheduled) areas,* Bharatiya Adimjati *Sevak Sangh,*Delhi, 1953, 129-134.

Vyas, A.N., "Fifteen Years of Progress of Tribal Education in Orissa", *Vanyajati, 1963. 11(2), 51-64.*

Vyas, N.N., "Banharas: The Merchantile Nomads of Rajasthan", Tribe, 1967, 3 (2).

Vyas, N.N. *"The Bhils on the Border of Rajasthan-An Emerging Situation"* (Read in the *Seminar on Tribal Situation in India,* Indian Institute of Advanced Study, Simla), 1969.

Vyas, N.N., "Trends of Change among the Bhil's of Rajasthan", *Tribe'* 1966, 3(1), 1-3.

Vyas, N.N. and Choudhary N.D., "Forest Co-Operatives and Change Among the Tribes", *Tribe,* 1969, 5(4).

Vyas , N.N. Mann, R.S. and Chaudhary N.D., "Rajasthan Bhills", *Udaipur Manikyalal Verma Tribal Research Training Institute,* 1978.

Waddel, L.A., "Note on the Poisoned Arrows of the Akas" *Journal of the anthropological Institute,* 1895, 24 (57).

Waler, G.D., "Garo Manugacture of Bark Cloth", *Man* 1927, 27 (5).

Watt, G., "The Aborigional Tribes of Manipur", *Journal of the Anthropological Institute,* Vol. XVI, (1887), pp. 346-70.

Wilde, Mrs. Frank., "The Kukis and Nagas of the North Cachar Hills, Assam", *Women of all Nations* (London 1909), Vol. 11. pp. 575-84.

Wilkinson T.S., "The Functional Significance of Ghotual Nomencalture", in Balaratnam (ed.) *Anthropology on the March,* Social Science Association, Madras, 1953, 315-319.

Wood, Browne, "Extracts from a Report of a Journey into the Naga Hills in 1944", *Journal of Asiatic Society of Bengal,* Vol. XIII, pt. 2 (1884), pp. 771-85.

Woodhrope, R.G., "Extract from the Narrative Report of the Lt. R.G. Woodthorpe", *General Report on the Topographical Survey of India for the* Season 1874-5. App. 53-63, Description of Lohotes and Aos.

Woodhrope, R.G., "Extract from the Narrative Report of the Naga Hills and Lakhimpur Expeditionary Survey Party", *General Reprot on the Operation of the Survey of India,* 1876-7.

Woodhrope, R.G., "Naga Hills Exploration Report on the Survey Operation in the Naga Hills 1875-6" *General Report on the Topographical Surveys of India,* 1875-6.

Woodhrope, R.G., "Notes Descriptive of the 'Country and People in Eastern and Eastern Naga Hills", *General Reprot of the Topographical Surveys of India,* 1874-5. App. 63-8.

Woodhrope, R.G., "Note on the Wild Tribes Inhabiting the So-called Naga Hills on our North-East Frontier of India", *Journal of the Anthropological Institute*, Vol. XI (1882). pp. 56-72. 196-212.

Yambem, Sanamani, "Nupi-Lan : Manipur Women's Agitation-1939" *Economic and Political Weekly*, Xi, 1976, 8. 325-330.

Young, A.W., "A Jewis Harpe in Assam", *Journal of the Royal Asiatic Society of Bengal,* Vol. IV (N.S. 1908), pp. 233-7.

Yule, H., "Notes on the Khasia Hills and People", *JASB*, Vol. XIII, No. 63, 1844.

Zimmermarr, R., "The Khandalla Katharis", *Journal of the Anthropological Society of Bombay,* 1921-24, 154-172.

Zustishi, G.L., "Preliminaries Regarding Applied Research Among Backward Classes", *Vanyajati*, 1959, 6(3).